About the author

D0784643

David Marfleet is the founder and Director of Giving the Best, a fundraising and development consultancy that specialises in advising small and medium sized charities. As he says in this book, *'Not many of us who call ourselves professional fundraisers planned our careers to end up this way. We morphed into the trade.'*

In his case, he spent the 1970s as an Army officer, serving as a paratrooper and helicopter pilot during the difficult years of 'the Troubles' in Northern Ireland. The 80s saw David Marfleet living in the jungles of New Guinea working as a missionary pilot. In 1990, he was awarded the prestigious Helicopter Association International *Pilot of the Year Award* for his part in a dramatic rescue operation following a devastating earthquake that hit the highlands of Irian Jaya.

His biography covering those exhilarating years was told in *Wings Like Eagles* by Clive Langmead, published by Lion Publishing, which sold over 120,000 copies.

A Member of the Institute of Fundraising, David Marfleet has many years of extensive experience at senior management and board level in the voluntary sector and has recently retired as the Chairman of an international NGO. He is a much sought-after conference speaker and trainer.

When not helping good causes become even better, he relaxes by bird watching, growing his own vegetables, sampling Real Ale, and running half-marathon races. He and his wife, Mary, have four adult children and are active members of a Baptist church in Kent.

Giving the Best
PO Box 453
Tonbridge
Kent
TN9 9EN
www.givingthebest.co.uk

GROW YOUR OWN
CHARITY

Down-to-earth essentials for managing good causes

David Marfleet

Matador
5 Weir Road
Kibworth Beauchamp
Leicester LE8 0LQ, UK
Tel: (+44) 116 279 2299
Fax: (+44) 116 279 2277
Email: books@troubador.co.uk
Web: www.troubador.co.uk/matador

ISBN 978 1848766 044

British Library Cataloguing in Publication Data
A catalogue record for this book is available from the British Library.

Typeset in 11pt Garamond by Troubador Publishing Ltd, Leicester, UK
Printed and bound in the UK by TJ Internation, Padstow, Cornwall

Matador is an imprint of Troubador Publishing Ltd

MIX
Paper from
responsible sources
FSC
www.fsc.org
FSC® C013056

This book is dedicated to
all those who dream about making the world a better place;
but especially to Mary,
who has helped me translate many dreams into reality.

" People should be queueing up to work
with you "
                    T. Adams 2011

Contents

Acknowledgments

The word 'charity' comes from the Latin *caritas,* meaning '*love*' or '*affection*'. My opening chapter reminds us that 'charity begins at home', so I have ample justification for thanking those nearest and dearest to me for all the '*caritas*' and tireless support I have received while writing this book.

For Mary, who has been my lifelong inspiration and encourager, I owe immeasurable thanks, especially for helping me to launch and run our company, *Giving the Best*. Other members of my family were involved in the production of this book too. My son Jon designed the cover, whilst my brother Andrew added some scholarly editorial guidance. My father – Sidney – who bequeathed to me so many worthwhile values during his lifetime – gave me the garden fork featured on the cover. He would have been thrilled to see it put to such good use here, although I don't ever remember seeing him use it for its proper purpose!

But there are others beyond the immediate family without whom this book would not have happened; among them are David Longley, Clive Langmead at Langmedia, Bob Moffett at Panahpur, Debra Allcock Tyler at DSC, Terry Compton and the publishing team at Matador. Each has added their own professional expertise.

But the main thanks go to all my many clients from literally hundreds of worthwhile causes, whose individual stories have contributed to making this book real. Without them the world would have a lot less *caritas*.

David Marfleet
December 2010

Foreword

In my capacity as Chair of the Small Charities Coalition and CEO of the Directory of Social Change, it is my privilege to work with a large number of small charities from inception to reality. And I know the excitement, energy, passion and hope that individuals pour into their causes.

But sadly, that passion is so often wasted when the charity fails because the individuals involved didn't fully understand the huge challenges they were about to face.

Running a charity is an enormous responsibility. The consequences of failure are potentially serious. It's not like setting up a small business where, if the business fails, the worst thing that happens is that people lose their jobs, sad though that is. If your charity fails then usually there is some person or cause that suddenly finds themselves bereft of support and/or help. So making it successful is so much more critical. It has profound consequences if, for example, you create a charity to serve young homeless people, build up those individuals by giving them support and hope, and then suddenly have to close down the service because you haven't properly thought through how you are going to get your resources to enable the service to continue.

So it is critical that you get sound, sensible advice before you begin. And there is a great deal of advice available about running a charity – quite literally thousands of books, articles on the internet, and so on. However, in my experience, much of the advice is either completely incomprehensible, in which case you are unable to take the right decisions, or the risks are so over-stated that people become fearful. And when people are afraid it becomes harder for them to take balanced risk assessments and make good decisions.

This book does not fall into those categories. It is grounded, sensible advice, that tells you the basics of what you need to know, in a way that is easy to understand and more importantly, easy to implement.

There are never any guarantees of success when you start a charitable organisation. There are always *'the slings and arrows of outrageous fortune'* to contend with.[1] But you stand a much better chance if you follow some basic steps. This book gives you an essential grounding in what you need to know. Enjoy, follow the advice – and may your charity thrive.

Debra Allcock Tyler
Chair, Small Charities Coalition
Chief Executive, Directory of Social Change

1 Charity begins at home – and it's probably yours

'Strive not to be a success, but rather to be of value.'
Albert Einstein

Not what I expected to find

I stumbled on Lisa's blog site by mistake – as you do when Google directs you to something you don't need. I should have quickly hit the 'back' arrow but I was gripped by her opening question:

'I'd like to form and register a charity for a cause close to my heart. Where do I begin?'

My mind raced with the myriad of things I wanted to ask her and warn her about. From those few words, I already knew so much about her. As far as I am aware, I have never met Lisa, but I do know hundreds of passionate men and women just like her. Perhaps you are someone like her, which is why you have started to read this.

Something must be done!

Somewhere, somehow, you have been moved by a personal experience and driven to wonder 'if only someone had been there to help'. Maybe a loved-one was tragically taken from you or, during a gap-year trip overseas, you encountered poverty and injustice on a scale you could never have imagined.

You are not the sort of person who just sits there pondering about problems. Something had to be done! So there and then you resolved to set it up – you were not sure what 'it' was. A trust? A charity? A social enterprise? You didn't want to change the World – just that part of it where you felt you could make a real difference – meeting the needs of a few of those desperate people, preserve something of intrinsic value, or headline an injustice. You are about to initiate something really worthwhile.

1

Reality sets in

But the initial euphoria of 'birthing' your own cause – seeing your new home-made website go live, or meeting with a group of friends soon to be ennobled with the title of 'Trustees' – may soon have given way to the harsh reality that, let's face it, you haven't a clue what to do next. You started off with some great ideas, but now, with your very own train set, you suddenly realise there is a whole lot more to running a railway than laying down the tracks. Your passion for the lost and needy is being quickly swamped by having to fill in forms for Her Majesty's Revenue and Customs, organising board meetings, or, worst of all, come up with some ideas for that dreaded fundraising. Because you now know you need money. Real money. A lot more than you have in your personal 'good cause' savings account, plus a fiver or two from friends. And this is all before starting to achieve any of the charitable aims which inspired you in the first place.

Where you make a difference

Your real skills and your motivation are probably rooted somewhere in what the charity sector calls '*service delivery*' – the real front-line work that the organisation was created for in the first place. What the real business is about. But your charity is *not* a business. Businesses are set up for one reason only – to make a profit. Charities need money – and some might engage in trading to make that money – but the money is only a tool they will use to serve the ultimate beneficiaries: to do 'what is says on the tin'. But you need to be *business-like* in the way you run your charity, or else you will find that you are not able to deliver that service very efficiently. Maybe you will never deliver anything really worthwhile at all.

Who gets the largest slice of the pie?

There are nearly 200,000 registered charities in the UK.[1] When most people think of charities they normally imagine large, well-run organisations such as *Lifeboats* or *Oxfam*. The large charities have the best profiles, and they can afford multi-media advertising and nationwide appeals. It is to them that journalists will turn when they need a spokesperson to comment on voluntary sector news items. They are the ones who (somewhat unfairly, in my opinion) get all the profile at major sporting events such as the London Marathon. However, the vast majority of charitable work done in the UK is carried out by small organisations.

And they are often struggling to get by. They are frequently overwhelmed by the needs around them, but because they don't have the income to meet those needs, they continue to scratch the surface of the problem.

According to Patrick Cox, founder of the *Small Charities Coalition*, 70% of all income in the voluntary sector goes to the largest 2% of charities, while the ten largest charities receive a quarter of the total money given to charity in the UK. That is heartbreaking news if you are running something small, relatively new and virtually unknown. All you need is just a *little* more of the pie! And you seem to be working as hard as humanly possible to get it. You feel you are moving forward through thick treacle, or not moving at all.

How will this book help me?

I genuinely believe that most small charities do not need to be stuck in this way; they just need to be helped up the first couple of rungs on the ladder. This book is aimed at founders and trustees of smaller charities who have 'hit the brick wall' and don't know what to do next. I want to introduce you to some basic concepts that I have found are a *must* when it comes to running a voluntary organisation. They will be *business-like,* but there will be no jargon, I promise. Some of them are well-tried and tested principles that have served many organisations well over the years. Others will be new concepts that I have developed while working at a senior level for international charities and, in more recent years, while serving many small organisations like yours, as a consultant. None of it will be 'rocket science' – just good common sense that will help you to deliver the goods.

Back to basics

This book is also designed to be a tool for those who have inherited the leadership of a small charity and are wondering why it is not working as well as it ought to. By going back to first principles, you may well discover essentials that the original founders had overlooked. It is not a high-flying, management-speak text book. I have deliberately crafted it to be an entry-level manual with some basic ideas of how to run a charity successfully and sustainably. Nor is it a 'Beginner's Guide to Fundraising' – there are plenty of those around, some of which I will recommend later. Fundraising is not usually the root of your problem, though, despite the fact that it may look as if it is to your frustrated trustees.

Not what it appears to be

Most of my clients come to me for help with fundraising because they are struggling financially. However, before I start evaluating their fundraising potential, there are usually a few strategic issues that need to be straightened out first. And by strategic, I mean the bigger picture, the overall planning. Issues that may well have caused the financial crisis in the first place. One leading management consultancy has this on its website:

'In over 29 years, never has the presented problem turned out to be the real organizational problem.' [2]

You may think that lack of working income is what is holding you back – I very much doubt if that is the real issue for you. There is probably something much more strategic that we need to deal with first.

Practical advice

So this is a practical look at some of *those* important questions. The ones you will need to answer *before* you start fundraising. If you put into practice some of the things I am suggesting in these pages you really should see positive results. I have seen it happen many times. And there is no great magic or mystery to it, I assure you. But it is surprising how something which may seem simple and obvious when highlighted may have been missed out simply because you have been trying to keep all your charity plates spinning at once.

Do not be discouraged. The world wants more people like you, and you need to be reaching your full philanthropic potential. The following chapters are intended to get you going in the right direction. Do not let go of the passion that brought you to this point in the first place. It is that passion that will be required to see you through the challenges that undoubtedly lie ahead.

Way to go!

In September 1942, an unknown clergyman, Canon Theodore Milford, gathered a group of friends together in a church hall in Oxford to discuss how they could send food parcels through the Allied blockade of

Nazi-occupied Greece. And the rest is *not just* history. The development of Oxfam from that meagre 'Oxford Committee for Famine Relief' is a story of passion and much hard work by the founder and those who came after him. They started out with many of the same frustrations and disappointments that you are now going through. But they eventually got it together. And so can you.

---

1 Including England and Wales, and Scotland.
2 http://www.emacassessments.com

The shape of things to come

'Before everything else, getting ready is the secret of success.'
Henry Ford

Powered by passion

Most charities are founded by people with a passion for the *service delivery*. These people are motivated by wanting to make a difference, to support a worthy cause, and usually have first-hand experience and a high level of skill in their area of concern. Parents whose children are suffering from a rare disease will often form charities to support others in their situation. Horticulturalists may have a burden for improving crops in a developing nation. Former soldiers have founded organisations that support war veterans. I was introduced to the charity sector when I worked as a pilot for a Christian organisation which was originally established by ex-wartime airmen and women who wanted to use their flying skills for church and development work in the post-war developing world.

Struggling

It is my experience that such founders are usually very competent in their own area of expertise. They are so good in fact, that the work of the charity initially blossoms, and that is when the problems often start. They quickly realise that doing accounts on the back of an envelope on the kitchen table is not good enough. The friends who paid for that initial shipment of mosquito nets all need thanking – but the spreadsheet with all their names and addresses is on the old laptop which is now running too slowly. And the girl who had originally said she would stuff those envelopes for you has been offered a full-time job elsewhere.

'If only one of the other trustees could help…?' Does this sound familiar?

Critical support

Numerous small charities have found that although they have a *passion* for their purpose and vision, and exhibit real *excellence* in their core work, the *critical support* functions that they need to develop in order to keep the charity functioning are pretty chaotic, to be honest. They are typically weak in one or more of the following areas:

Governance. In terms of running a charity, 'governance' is all about the legal and financial responsibility that your board of trustees (sometimes called 'directors') has. They are called 'trustees' because the general public is *trusting* them with, and will hold them accountable for, all the charity's assets. They are also holding 'in trust' the original charitable purpose – in short, the board is ultimately responsible for ensuring that the work you were set up to do is done effectively and efficiently, and they will be held accountable by law for doing so. Scary stuff!

Financial management. Good bookkeeping is not just about paying the bills on time, or making sure that there is enough cash to pay wages. One of the strengths of being a charity is that there is integrity and openness about the way the charity manages the money that it has been entrusted with. So you will need to be able to keep accounts that conform to 'best practice' and that are available for inspection or audit.

Strategic planning. Strategy is one of those buzz words that people in the business world throw around – sometimes without really understanding the full meaning. It's about how you intend to reach your ultimate goal. This is the big picture, not the minuscule detail. Derived from a Greek word meaning 'General', *'strategy'* has military connotations. *Tactics* dictate how troops will capture a particular hill, but *strategy* will plan for how an army will win the war. You will need a strategic plan if you are going to win your war against all the gremlins that are currently holding you back.

Information technology. Computers, internet, etc. Elizabeth Fry, Thomas Barnardo, William Booth and countless others set up flourishing charities over 100 years ago without a silicon chip in sight. But you can't do that today. I remember when computers were an item of luxury, at best convenience. Today they are a vital necessity. When they go wrong – well, we all know about that, don't we?

Fundraising. No need to explain this one! I wish there was a better term for it, because it implies that somehow money can be grown or raised like a family. The process of fundraising is not about money at all, it's about *people*. People who are invited to enter a relationship, and in so doing, discover the thrill of generosity.

Donor development. Vitally important, but so often missed completely. If your fundraising is limited to rattling a tin or selling a few raffle tickets, you will only collect cash, but you will not collect the long-term donors necessary to ensure that you will still be in business this time next year. Donors need to be developed, like any relationship. And that comes though an investment of time and effort.

Marketing. No, I am not talking about advertising or selling. Those are just two small ingredients in the so-called 'marketing mix'. A marketing plan for your charity will look at your *product* (in your case, the work or service you provide) and ask what it will take to convince the general public that they want it, need it, can afford it, and that it will do what you say it will do. Fundraising and *marketing* go hand in hand. You cannot do one without the other. They are the Ant and Dec of charity work – you never see one without the other, and you probably don't even know which one is which.

Needs must...?

You are probably beginning to realise that there is more to this than you thought – you are right! But don't despair. We are going to unpack all of these issues as we go along. But let's back up a moment and ask a really risky, shock horror question. Assuming you are at an early stage and have not started any of the charity registration process, let me ask...

Do you really need to form another charity?

I am not trying to catch you out. It really does need to be asked. The Charity

Commission, in online guidance to anyone planning to register a charity in England and Wales, gives the following advice:

'There are more than 190,000 registered charities, working throughout the UK and overseas, which undertake an extremely wide range of work. It is very likely that a charity already exists which is doing the kind of work which you would like to carry out, and there may be one working in your area of the country. We suggest that you think about whether it would be better to offer your services to, or combine with, an existing charity. It is usually less effective to have several organisations trying to carry out the same work in the same place, and it duplicates running costs.'[1]

You might save yourself a lot of unnecessary heartache if you took that little piece of wisdom to heart! Remember the ultimate purpose of your charitable effort is the well-being of the beneficiaries, not your own feel-good factor or your expanded ego in handing out business cards with 'International Director' printed all over them. The people you have identified as being in need of your help might be better assisted by you offering your skills to another organisation. Of course it might be that after a couple of years working with an established agency you feel that the sector could cope with another charity. You might want to set up something to specialise in an area not covered by anyone else and you will be glad that you gained knowledge and experience first. Do not reinvent the wheel. But if you want a wheel that serves a slightly different purpose, it will have been a lot less painful for you to have completed the research and development stage at someone else's factory. Learn by the mistakes of others – they may have already been down the road you want to walk, and can give you some excellent advice about the conditions under foot.

My 'Triangle of Sustainability'

But let's go back to the dilemma of the emerging charity. This is where I need to introduce you to my *Triangle of Sustainability*. In order for a charity of any size to achieve sustainability, the relationship between four groups of people and the way they interact with each other is vital.

The most important group of people in your organisation are the very people you set out to help in the first place – the *Beneficiaries*. But you can only help them if you have sufficient financial resources generated from the second group who we can call the *Supporters*. The process of helping the beneficiaries has to be managed, so another two groups come into play here, the *Management* and the *Trustees*. How these four groups of people work together will determine how efficiently you can grow as an organisation. These four groups and the vital roles they play must be kept in tension with each other, and must develop at the same pace if sustainability is to be achieved.

We can best illustrate this diagrammatically. Figure 1 shows how the **Service Delivery** (beneficiaries), **Governance** (trustees), and **Fundraising** (supporters) are all held in equal tension by the **Executive** (management).

Interestingly, I originally drew this diagram with Governance at the apex. I had automatically defaulted towards hierarchical thinking! Actually, as we have just noted, the most important facet of any charity – the sole reason it exists – is the delivery of the service to the ultimate beneficiaries. So I have redrawn it to emphasis that the trustees and supporters are servants of the beneficiaries and not the other way round.

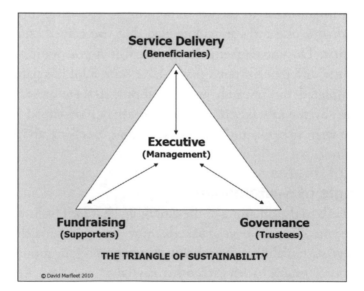

Figure 1

It is an equilateral triangle, with equal sides and equal angles, and no one side or angle must be allowed to increase in capacity out of pace with the others. Have you ever tried to build a tower out of a pack of playing cards? You have to make sure that each layer has the same number of cards, exactly positioned to equally bear the load of the card you are about to place on the top. If you don't, it wobbles at the first breath of wind, and quickly collapses. My *Triangle of Sustainability* is just like that. Get the structure out of proportion, and it will collapse. When applying this to your charity, by structure I mean the people, the roles they play, and their relationship to each other in the organisation. The interdependence and mutual accountability of the four key functions shown in the Triangle are only complete as a whole structure – a triangle with only two sides is a contradiction in terms. But the Triangle also begs strategic questions to be asked of each of the functions, such as 'Who?' and 'How?'

Strategy and structure

So to make your charitable organisation sustainable – to withstand the storms that are inevitably coming your way – you will need not only a *strategy*; you will need a *structure* within the organisation to deliver it. People need to be in the right jobs, in the right relationship with each other, and they need to have the competencies to perform the tasks required of them. Without that, you can write all the strategy papers you like, but they will be unlikely to help you achieve the goals they prescribe.

These four functions could be seen as *Critical Success Factors*, because each of them is critical to the success of the organisation. We will come back to this again in later chapters.

Keeping the plates spinning

Unless you are totally unlike any other charity that has been formed, you and a few friends are probably trying hard to fulfil all the core functions of the Triangle, but perhaps in a haphazard or crisis management way. Fire-fighting instead of formulating and functioning. Working furiously at one thing and then turning away to deal with something else which has just come up. Just being happy to keep all the plates at least spinning in some fashion.

But for the moment, take a good look at the Triangle and the Critical Success Factors (CSFs). See how they interact, how they work together and how they provoke questions – and demand answers – to balance up the Triangle. You must plan strategically to keep the structure of the organisation – the people, the roles and the work they all do – in balance.

Band aid

Talking of triangles, maybe you see your work rather like the solo busker on the tube station, or perhaps more realistically, a one-man band, trying to beat time with a cymbal tied to your knee, a drum on your back while strumming on a banjo. I want to move you on towards being more like a four-piece band or chamber orchestra.

For several years, one of my sons played in a professional rock band. I can listen to one of his CDs now and be proud of what he achieved as a musician, as an accomplished bass player. But only he really knows what it took to hone the individual skills of each member of the band until they could work together, in a studio, to produce a balanced masterpiece of sound. The producer had to mix those individual elements to balance drums against bass, vocals against keyboard etc. It all had to be professionally managed and the record label held them accountable for delivery. A far cry from the jam sessions they used to have in our back room in the early days. But the end result was well worth the effort.

We will return in Chapter 4 to look in detail at each of the individual elements of the Triangle, how to get each one of these CSFs correctly balanced, so that your charity will stand. It will sustain, it will grow, it will deliver!

But first we need to spend a little more time in deciding where we *are* really going.

---

1 www.charity-commission.gov.uk

3 Where do you want to sit?

Centre forward

Logic dictates that I should start at the top of the Triangle and work my way around, ending up in the central role of the *Executive* last of all. I am not going to do that. For a start, *Service Delivery* is what you are good at – that's probably not your main concern. I am going to jump straight in at the centre, to where you are sitting. You are after all, probably the 'Executive' by default, and you are almost certainly doing much, if not all, of the other core functions too.

Problems for the founder

Let me introduce you to a much-discussed ailment that can cripple the development of any young charity. It is called *'Founder Member Syndrome'*, or FMS. It is very common, but the good news is that prompt diagnosis brings you a long way towards the cure. See if you can recognise the symptoms...

Symptom Number One of FMS is when you are doing everything yourself. Everything except perhaps the one thing you are really good at – the service delivery of your charitable objective. The consultant ophthalmologist who spends all his time organising agendas for trustees' meetings and worrying about fundraising, and rarely has a chance to think about the eye clinic he has set up in Africa, is suffering from FMS. The reality is that while these other Critical Success Factors *do* have to be addressed, if they stop him delivering the real service, he needs to find someone else to help in those areas.

Out of Africa

One of my recent clients was a charity working to address the impact of AIDS

13

in Southern Africa. They have around 35 expat and national staff in seven countries throughout the continent. The work they are doing is incredible, but the workload always exceeds their capacity to deliver. They came to me for help when their resourcing failed to keep pace with the needs in Africa. It didn't take me long to realise the problem. Their *Triangle of Sustainability* was no longer working in equilibrium. Service delivery had taken off very successfully, but no one was responsible for fundraising, and their UK supporter base was virtually nonexistent. The three UK-based trustees were desperately trying to raise some much-needed cash, with no one to call on.

It is true that trustees have a very important role to play in fundraising but that is not their most important role. Governance is. In this particular case, the trustees were fulfilling the roles of the 'Executive' and, to an almost desperate extent, 'Resourcing', but were not looking at the bigger issues of strategic direction and proper governance. They had allowed the balance of the Triangle to shift quite significantly. And the natural outcome of this was *unsustainability*.

What we had to do was to bring things back into a more triangular shape by preparing a strategy that would strengthen the UK resourcing side of the charity, and I suggested appointing a part-time fundraiser (or at least someone who could make a start on implementing the trustees' fundraising ideas).

Keeping it in proportion
The key to keeping the Triangle sustainable is that you must not let any side develop out of proportion to the others. As we have seen, the usual problem is that the charitable work grows faster than you can resource it, not least because the founders are genuine experts at doing that work. But if any of the other areas – Governance or Fundraising – takes precedence over the Service Delivery to the extent that you are spending more time or donation income in these areas than on your charitable objects, then your operation will begin to run rough – and, in fact, you could even incur the wrath of the Charity Commission! While there are no hard and fast rules about how much you can spend on fundraising, governance and administration, I would suggest you should aim to show in your Annual Report to the Charity Commission at least 60-70% of your donated income being used for 'service delivery'.

Looking ahead

When I started writing this, I was advising a young woman who was passionate about setting up a children's charity in South East Asia. She was just bursting with ideas on fundraising and had produced an impressive website. I introduced her to the concept of the Triangle, and cautioned her that in the early days, she was most likely to be doing everything herself. However, even in this formative period, I said she ought to have in mind an embryonic structure which will allow her ultimately to concentrate on the care for orphaned children, while releasing others to govern and resource the new charity.

Wearing too many hats is bad for your head

Symptom Number Two of FMS is when the founder cannot decide what job he or she ought to be doing. Sometimes they want to be the Chair of the Board of Trustees and sometimes they want to be the Chief Executive. But most of all they want to be in charge of delivering the goods, in other words, being the 'front-end' of the charity and working with the ultimate beneficiaries, but do not want to let go of the controls when they have put so much into this personal enterprise.

The usual working model for how charities ought to be structured is that there is a Board of Trustees who are responsible for the overall legal, financial, and other governance issues. One of them will be the Chair (we will expand on the function and duties of Board in the next chapter). The Board appoints a Chief Executive, or Executive Director, to be responsible for the day-to-day running of the organisation. The Chief Executive, in turn, hires the staff necessary for all the working functions of the organisation, according to policies set by the Board. OK, that's the theory. But in practice, it is usually the founder who forms the first Board and calls all the shots. So, if you are the founder, where do you want to sit?

I have been stressing in this book that wearing multiple hats is fine at the outset, but however good at multi-tasking you are, it is vital that you have an 'exit strategy' in mind. You need to decide right now which of these key roles you eventually want to settle into, and plan for that accordingly.

Un-musical chairs

Being Chair and Chief Executive might work in the corporate sector but is definitely the wrong working model for charities. The Board not only appoints the Chief Executive; they hold him or her accountable for the daily operation of the charity. *You cannot be accountable to yourself.* The whole purpose of being a charity and enjoying the protection afforded by charity law is to have checks and balances in place to create transparency and confidence with donors and other stakeholders.

It is possible to be Chief Executive and be responsible for the service delivery, but there are drawbacks to this too. I worked my way up to acting CEO of an international charity and found that my time was largely taken up with issues of Health and Safety, employment regulations, board meetings and other important, but not very exciting, activities. If your skills are more geared towards the front-line work, you might be better off looking for someone who enjoys management to do these things for you.

It all sounds good in theory, and I expect more than a few readers are saying 'Yes, I must do that!' When it comes to implementing such decisions, it can be a huge step handing over the reins and the authority for the organisation you have conceived, birthed and raised as your own.

But it's *my* party!

Symptom Number Three of FMS is when you do not trust anyone else to run 'your organisation' instead of you. Maybe the founder has appointed some friends who share their passion to be the initial trustees. But who is really calling the shots? Do the trustees simply 'rubber stamp' all the ideas the founder comes up with or is there some objective accountability in place? Even if the founder is not the Chair of the Board, it is often hard for the new trustees to really give direction to a strong-willed founder.

'All those in favour...'

Let's be honest – if someone invites you to become a trustee of their new charity, part of their dream, and they are running the show in a very hands-on style, you are very unlikely to stand up and disagree with the agenda they are proposing, are you? This scenario is very common, and it makes a mockery of the whole process really, because the very checks and balances the system was supposed to provide have just gone out of the window.

A few months ago, I was running a governance training seminar for the trustees of a new charity which is working among war trauma victims in Africa. The founder is a very gifted and passionate lady who could fit equally well into any of the role functions of the Triangle. After we had discussed these very issues at some length, she confided in me that she had decided that she must relinquish her role on the board to concentrate on being a successful Chief Executive. I told her that this would be a courageous step to take, but probably the right one. It has not been easy for her to surrender control of the organisation's direction to others, but so far it has worked out brilliantly because the relationship between her and the new Chair has been one of deep mutual respect and trust.

It is sometimes right to hand over control to others once the initial set-up is complete. It requires a different skills set to manage a start-up than it does to run an organisation.[1] *Handing over the responsibility is fine, but with it must go authority and ownership for the task or project too.*

Going, going, but not quite gone

One of my long-standing clients recently went through the process of appointing a new Executive Director on the retirement of the founder who had held this post for over 10 years. He had done a great job in birthing and developing the work. He had a strong Board which supported him well, and he was looking forward to handing over the reins to someone new. His successor was eventually recruited and she took her place 'at the helm'.

In recognition of his hard work and devotion to the charity, the Board gave the founder the honorary title of 'President', but failed to spell out any job description or 'executive limitation' for this role. To make matters worse, the head office was in a barn conversion adjoining the founder's own property. You can imagine what happens can't you! With the best will in the world, the President frequently 'pops into the office to see how things are going.' Because these two, both very gifted leaders, have different management styles and different ideas on how things should be run, it is a powder keg just waiting to blow up. It is an unworkable situation for both the incoming new Executive Director and the President/Founder.

Take a look at yourself

This is not an isolated incident. It is very common. I helped found a local community group once, in the village where we live. I love starting new initiatives, but once they are up and running, I like to hand over to someone else. Eventually we appointed a full-time leader, but the members of the group would often come to me as the founder, bypassing the new leadership. I got on really well with the leader in question, he was a close friend, but I had not realised that my very presence in the group was undermining his authority. The only solution was for me to completely withdraw from the group in order for the new leadership to function properly. There was no big scene – no throwing the toys out of the pram, I simply explained to all concerned that we needed to move on in order that the organisation could flourish.

Paul Martin, a leading charity lawyer, advises:

'Most charities at some stage have to face the fact that the entrepreneurial single-minded visionary leadership that gave birth to the organisation is not the only skill that is required to take the organisation forward. Sooner or later, the qualities of team building, delegation, participatory management and accountability are those that have to be developed in the charity, if the work is to be sustained and the baton passed on to a new generation.' [2]

If, as the founder, you are more comfortable in one particular area of job function, you should develop a strategy that will lead to you moving into that role and appointing others to take on the other responsibilities. Remember that this process will be hard for everyone involved, not just you, and will take some effort by all involved until everything is running smoothly.

Should a cause die with its founder?

Before leaving the issue of the founder, we ought to just mention what might happen when the founder moves on or 'passes on'. There are basically two main reasons why a charity might be founded. Either someone is deeply burdened or concerned about a cause or they realise they have gifts and training in a certain area which they feel may be of benefit, perhaps unique benefit, to others. German-born George Müller was famous for starting his work among orphans in Bristol in the 1830s. This local churchman was not particularly gifted in the area of social care but felt that something just had to be done following a cholera outbreak in the port in 1832. Their parents having died, hundreds of young orphans were left to fend for themselves on the streets. So he did something. The American evangelist Billy Graham is a good example of the other type – his 'Billy Graham Evangelistic Association' was set up originally to facilitate his highly popular international preaching tours.

Drifting off course

So what happens when the founder is no longer active? A lot will depend upon which of these two models the charity was built upon. When Müller died, the needs of the street children were just as great, and others continued the work for years after his death. The Purpose of the charity in this case was still valid. In the case of a charity that has been set up to facilitate an individual's philanthropy or ministry, unless a successor steps up to take the founder's place, the charity may as well cease or it must change its original Purpose and Charitable Objects. I know of a couple of charities where the trustees are struggling to define their Purpose because the original founder has died, and there has been 'strategic drift' which has caused them to lose their way. They are still doing some 'good work', but it is questionable if they would have founded a charity today just for that purpose. They ought to consider winding it up.

Mutually accountable

When I introduced the Triangle, I stressed that mutual accountability, checking and being checked by each other – but in a supportive, not hostile way – was a requirement of the structure. Mutual accountability breeds trust, and where there is trust *with* accountability, there is confidence in delegating authority and responsibility. This is the key. The trustees hold the Chief Executive accountable, but in return, the CEO, indeed the whole organisation, expects the trustees to govern with integrity and to keep the vision alive and on track. Those responsible for the service delivery will be held accountable for meeting the needs of the charity's ultimate beneficiaries, but they can also expect the fundraisers to deliver the agreed resources to enable them to succeed. Those responsible for raising funds will have been given realistic targets that they are required to meet, but they too can expect project descriptions and reports from 'the field' in order to meet donor expectations. When the whole organisation is functioning in this kind of balanced mutuality, sustainability is much easier to achieve. Donors and end-users alike have their expectations met. And the Chief Executive can sleep at night, secure in the confidence of the trustees, and vice versa.

So, if you are the founder, where do you see your future role in the organisation? Chief Executive might well be the most natural and logical role for you. Maybe as we move around the Triangle you might begin to identify another area that motivates you more.

---

1 See Chapter 11 for more thoughts on Belbin Team Roles.
2 Martin (2008), p.49.

4

Trust me...
I'm a Board Member

'In order to change the world, you have to get your head together first.'
Jimi Hendrix

Choosing your Board

You are probably itching to get on to some ideas about fundraising, but remember, I said there was quite a lot of critical spadework to be done before we can talk about your income mix. Appointing and running your Board of Trustees is one of them. Maybe you have already realised that your relationship with your trustees is a hot issue – one of the plates you are struggling to keep spinning.

So who *should* be your trustees? We have already said that it is quite common for the founder to approach close friends and family to become the first trustees. In many cases, the people involved share the passion and the vision of the founder, but have sometimes not realised the legal and moral responsibilities they are about to take on. I work with many agencies where the initial trustees have included members of the clergy and other church leaders. These are fine godly women and men who are committed to the practical expression of their faith through charitable service. I suspect though, that some of them have been selected more for their godliness than their competencies in governance. Don't get me wrong – I believe godliness is a pretty vital ingredient of life and, sadly, in short supply today – but being godly does not mean you can automatically walk on water when it comes to running a charity.

If you as the founder are looking for people to serve on your Board, think of the core competencies you might need, and try to identify people who might have those skills – the kind of people who will think strategically, bring business-like contributions and who will be committed to some hard work. Avoid people who enjoy putting forward their own ideas at the expense of listening to others. You will soon tire of those sorts at your meetings.

Having a heart

Above all, I would say that in order to serve on any Board, you have to be *excited* about the cause. Board meetings can be pretty heavy at the best of times, but unless you are really going to enjoy making a contribution to the end results, don't bother joining up. Board meetings should never turn out to be 'bored' meetings! I have been asked to serve on Boards several times where I knew I had the skills and could make a contribution, but I turned down the request because my heart was not in the cause. If your heart is not there, you will never give your best.

Paul Martin also makes an interesting point in that it is not advisable for both a husband and wife (or two other persons from the same household) to be trustees of the same charity! Imagine a situation where the founder is in effect the Chief Executive, and close family members make up the majority of the Board. Although technically legal, this situation is pretty unworkable in practice. The Board holds the Chief Executive accountable and must at all times make decisions in the best interests of the charity. It is very unlikely that the family in question would vote to remove the CEO from office if the rest of the Board felt he or she were incompetent or acting other than in the best interests of the charity![1]

A couple of years ago, the Charity Commission questioned a registration that I was filing for a client, where family members made up the majority of the Board. They were asked to appoint more independent trustees so that the family would be in the minority, before registration was approved.

What does the Board *actually* do?

The Charity Commission publishes an excellent little booklet *'Being a Trustee'* which is also available as a download on its website.[2] This is a good starting point for deciding what sorts of people might make successful trustees for you.

You may also find the following list helpful. I have put it together from various sources over the years.[3]

10 Key Board responsibilities

1. Set and maintain Purpose, Values and Vision
The Board of Trustees is responsible for establishing the essential Purpose or mission of the organisation. It is also responsible for guarding Vision and core Values.

2. Ensure compliance with the governing document
The governing document is the rulebook for the organisation. The organisation's activities must comply with its Charitable Objects.

3. Help develop strategy
The Board helps the Chief Executive Officer develop long-term strategic plans by determining the end goals for the organisation.

4. Establish and monitor policies
The Board creates policies to govern organisational activity and to protect the organisation and those who work for it.

5. Ensure accountability and compliance and that all the organisation's activities are legal
The Board should ensure that the organisation is accountable to:

- The Charity Commission (or Office of the Scottish Charity Regulator, OSCR; or the Charity Commission for Northern Ireland, CCNI)
- Her Majesty's Revenue and Customs
- Companies House (if it is a charitable company)
- Donors, beneficiaries, staff, volunteers, and other stakeholders.

6. Maintain proper fiscal oversight
The Board is responsible for effective management of the organisation's resources so it can meet its charitable objects. It must:

- Approve the annual budget
- Monitor spending
- Seek to minimise risk

7. Appoint, manage and support the Chief Executive
The Board appoints the Chief Executive and reviews his or her performance and salary.

8. Maintain effective Board performance
The Board takes steps to establish:

• Productive Board meetings
• Recruitment and induction processes for new trustees
• Regular performance reviews

9. Promote the organisation
Through its own behaviour, governance, and activities on behalf of the organisation, the Board enhances and protects the reputation of the organisation. Board members are ambassadors for the organisation.

10. Has overall responsibility for fundraising
The Board sets fundraising policies and, where appropriate, trustees use their own influence and contacts to secure major gifts.

Read this list again and ask yourself if the men and women you have on your Board of Trustees (or you have in mind to form your Board) have the competencies to fulfil these obligations. They might have many other skills and qualities, but if they are unable to act corporately to fulfil the above requirements, your Board will not function and the Triangle will start to collapse. They then become what Ken Burnett has described as 'an incompetent group of highly competent people'.[4]

Trustees must accept ultimate responsibility for everything the charity does. The buck really does stop here! They may delegate much of the day-to-day running of the organisation to the Executive and staff, but they cannot abdicate responsibility when things go wrong.

I have had the unfortunate experience of serving on Boards that had incompetent members, or worse, incompetent Chairs, and I have also served as part of an executive team that was being governed by ineffective or incompetent Board members. It can tear the soul out of an otherwise great organisation.

It is really difficult to find people who have the time, energy, competencies, and passion for your cause to serve on the Board; *but it is even harder to get rid of trustees you already have who don't have these prerequisites.*

Sitting not-so-pretty

So what can do you do about the trustees you would rather not have on your Board? The first essential is to make sure that your governing document limits the time a trustee is permitted to serve and outlines the procedures for re-election. If all else fails, you can look forward to having them retire!

The situation may warrant something being done before then though. This is where the skills and diplomacy of a good Chair come into play. The Chair should meet privately with any trustee who is being either ineffective or disruptive, and discuss the situation, gently but firmly pointing out that it is generally felt that they are no longer adding value to the Board process. It may well be that they are unhappy about being on the Board and would welcome the opportunity to bow out gracefully. The ultimate resort may well be the least desirable route, which is to vote the individual off. You would be well advised to take legal advice before 'rocking the boat' in this way.

Means to an End

I was for many years Chair of an international organisation working in Central Asia. We evolved a Board process where we adapted the methods of American author Dr John Carver. The Carver model distinguishes between the organisational goals, which Carver calls 'Ends', and the 'Means' which the organisation adopts to realise those 'Ends'. The Board determined the 'Ends' but it was the Director's job to decide what 'Means' he used to meet those 'Ends'. In practice, the Board and Director worked together on producing both the 'Ends' and the 'Means'. But we all had to learn a new way of thinking – we as the Board did not meddle with management issues. In turn, management expected the Board to set policies and direction.

The process was made even simpler by the fact that we set the Director's 'limitations' for each of the agreed 'Ends'. He could not exceed these limits. Whilst it might appear to be a negative approach, it was in fact very liberating, because he could do anything he wanted to do, as long as he stayed within the boundaries we had set, but otherwise being quite free to use creative thinking to achieve the 'Ends'. The Director knew exactly what was required and what was forbidden.[5]

Let me give you some examples of how it worked in practice. Early on in our development of this radical model of governance, I had tabled an agenda item as '*Annual salary review*', because we always did this around that time of year before approving the budget. We were well into our deliberations as to whether we could afford to give the staff a 2½% or 3% pay rise in line with current inflation, when one of my fellow trustees suddenly interjected, 'Wait a minute – this is not our responsibility. It's John's!' indicating the Executive Director on my right. 'As long as John stays within his Executive Limitations, one of which says that he may not exceed the agreed budget, he can pay his staff whatever he likes!'

Absolutely right, too! As a Board we only had one employee – the Executive Director. We decided his salary and terms of employment, but he was responsible for the rest of his team, because they are the 'Means' he chooses to help him accomplish his task. His task was to present us with a budget for approval. Part of that budget included how much he was going to spend on salaries. We would have questioned his figures if we were not confident that he had got it right, but we left the nitty-gritty to him.

Imagine a charity, for example, that is set up to provide computer training for ex-offenders. The standard of knowledge that each student might be able to eventually reach, and what the cost might be for providing that level of training, are 'Ends' issues, because they are about the impact the charity is going to have on the community it serves. So the Board should decide them. However, the choice over which software or textbooks to use, the qualifications required for teaching staff and the use of the training facilities available are all 'Means' issues, and they should be left to the Executive to decide.

Lines and limits

It's a paradigm shift from how most 'top-down' Boards like to function. Here are some of the other distinctives of how Carver's model works:

- The Board must always speak with unanimity. All Board decisions and policies must be completely supported by each and every Board member. The Board as a whole speaks with a unified voice only to the CEO/Director.

- The role of the Board is to develop policy. Board authority does not extend into management because it delegates management authority to the CEO/Director, and then empowers him/her to exercise authority commensurate with established policy.

- The function of the Board chair is not to supervise the CEO/Director, but to ensure the proper policy function of the Board.[6]

Where I personally diverge a little from Carver is that he believes that the Board should not be an advisory body but a 'commanding body', giving clear instructions, but not advice, to the CEO. I think it is a clear waste of trustees' experience and knowledge if they don't pass on some of those gems to the CEO. At the end of the day though, the CEO can choose whether to heed that advice or not. I had a very good working relationship with my Executive Director. He would frequently phone me for advice, particularly over fundraising issues, where he knew I had a lot to offer.

Big is not better

I am often asked how large a Board should be. It is a good question but one without a perfect answer. You need to have sufficient members to be able to work effectively, with the right balance of skills and experience. Small Boards are easy to manage, but can present problems if any one member is absent for a meeting. Your Trust Deeds or Articles of Association will prescribe how many trustees must be present to constitute a quorum. On the other hand, a large Board can become an ineffective cumbersome committee with everybody wanting to have a say on every point of order. The National Trust for Scotland was recently criticised in a strategic review for having no less than 87 Board members! The report called for an urgent review of their *'Byzantine governance structures'.* [7]

Getting the Board composition and function right is like laying out the foundations for a building. If you get it right, the building will stand strong against wind and weather. Get it wrong, and the construction will always suffer, particularly when under strain. The interface between CEO and the Board, and an understanding of how the Triangle of Sustainability works inter-relationally, is like the mortar that binds the brickwork of the structure to the concrete of the foundations.

It is a delicate business and few Boards are perfect! Even good Boards make mistakes – I have served on Boards where we sometimes got it wrong. You learn your best lessons from your mistakes and failures. But that's no excuse for putting up with a poorly-functioning Board.

1 Martin (2008), p.49.

2 www.charity-commission.gov.uk/

3 I cannot claim these are my original ideas. I have picked them up from a variety of publications and online sources, none of which I can remember now, but I use them frequently during seminars and presentations. If you recognise them as part of your original work, please contact me. I would be only too pleased to give credit to the original authors.

4 This is one Ken Burnett's oft-quoted tongue-in-cheek clichés, but see The Guardian, Society, 2 March 2006.

5 Carver (1997). Care should be taken, however, in adapting Carver's methodology in the setting of a UK charity. It is very much an American model. Ultimately, the Board is still responsible for everything the staff implements as part of the 'Means', and so careful reporting procedures must be put in place to ensure that trustees are aware of and approve all that happens within the charity.

6 Carver's Policy Governance Model in Nonprofit Organizations www.carvergovernance.com

7 Third Sector 17 August 2010, p.10.

5 Finding the funds

'Fundraising is not about money … it's about inspiring people to give.'
Ken Burnett

Fun or fundraising?

As we work round the *Triangle of Sustainability*, we must now look at the *Critical Success Factor* that we have labelled as 'Fundraising'. Maybe it would be a good idea to flick back to Chapter 2 momentarily to remind yourself what the Triangle looks like as we move on.

I have said all along that this is NOT a book about fundraising practices. But I do want to lay down some principles that will help you along the right track. When we get to Chapter 11, we will look at the task of selecting and managing your first in-house fundraiser. But for now we need to say something briefly about the possible sources of your *Income Mix*. Whole books have been devoted to each of these subjects; what follows here is intended to introduce you to some general principles you will need to consider.

Donors are *real people!*

You will no doubt already have a small list of friends who are supporting your work. It is vital that you take every opportunity to build this list. Finding these donors is not like just adding more 'Friends' on Facebook; names added to your database ultimately mean funds in your bank balance. In time, you will be able to calculate the direct benefit in £s for every name added to the database. But beware you do not fall into the trap of seeing your supporters only as names or numbers on a database. These are your loyal friends – you need their involvement at every level, not just their money. Treat them as close friends – we are going to talk more about this in the next chapter.

Say 'thank you'

Respect them. Protect their interests. Listen to their ideas and concerns. They are the lifeblood of all you do. Communicate with them regularly, not only when you need their money. Thank them personally every time they do make a donation, no matter how small the gift; it may have been a huge sacrifice to them. People give to charity for different reasons. Few will admit that they are motivated purely because they want to be appreciated. However, when they are thanked there is a 'feel good' factor which increases their relationship with the cause they have supported.

'Saying thank you to supporters is both an essential courtesy and a piece of enlightened self-interest that fundraisers forget at their peril.' [1]

You can buy lists of names from direct mail agencies, but it is my experience that this sort of prospecting rarely leads to long-term relationships. Instead, identify those who have a close affinity to your cause. The people who come to your Christmas Carol Service are probably interested in what you do. They haven't come just for the mince pies. The parents of that traumatised young soldier whose broken mind you are helping to rebuild understand the importance of what you are doing. Ask yourself 'How can we engage with these people more effectively? How can we enter into a deeper relationship with them? How can we 'scratch where they itch?'

Door-stepping and 'chuggers'

Face-to-face fundraising where agency staff are paid to recruit new donors on the street or on the doorstep are becoming increasingly controversial, but dare I say it, successful forms of donor acquisition. Most of us hate being accosted in the street to be asked if we would like to sign up for a £2 a month direct debit to a worthy cause. Despite the evidence that shows that this form of fundraising does bring in much needed instant cash, I would caution against a new charity considering this method.

Firstly, it is a very expensive form of donor acquisition – you could probably use the money more effectively elsewhere. Secondly, it only works for well-known charities, where the potential donor is already sympathetic to the cause. Lastly, the jury is still out as to whether it produces long-term relationships. The attrition rate of cancelled direct debit during the first year can make the whole exercise non-cost-effective. And of course, it is certainly not going to make you popular among the masses, which for the most part, are offended by these methods.

It is important to give your new donors choice. They may have signed up to receive news of your organisation at an event, they may have returned a coupon or insert in a mailing, they may be a friend of one of your existing supporters; but in each case they should receive a letter or email welcoming them to the organisation and asking them how they would like to be kept in touch with you. If someone is expecting the occasional newsletter and instead receives six 'begging letters' from you in the first year, you cannot expect to build a strong relationship.

Keep it cool

People under the age of, say, 30 prefer to receive news via email these days. They don't do hard copy – my nephew replied to a wedding invitation by SMS text recently! Give them the choice – communication by email is much more cost-effective anyway and properly handled, can be an effective form of fundraising. And it is much better for the environment!

We will return in the next chapter to the specifics of managing a 'high-value donor' programme. But for now, you need to consider *all* your donors as having high value. They are your friends; you need to value them as such.

Stay in touch

One of the most important ways to maintain a friendship is to stay in regular contact. I am writing this chapter in a hotel room while on business in Istanbul. Already today I have taken a mobile phone message from a daughter who wanted to check that I was watching England get humiliated at football (concerned about her father's stress levels, I think). I have sent a Facebook message to one of my sons serving in Afghanistan, and I have had a couple of Skype conversations with my wife who is holding the fort back home. These are people who are very dear to me – I find every way I can to communicate with them. Managing the process of communicating with your donors, too, is vital.

How we communicate with our supporters, and who takes the responsibility for it, are vital pieces of management planning. Hard copy direct mail is expensive and you need to make sure you are bringing added value to every piece of communication you produce.

The mighty mouse

One way to improve communication and keep your costs down is, of course, to make *electronic communication* your default method of staying in touch with donors. Of course, you are still going to need to have hard copy mailings for some of your supporters, but you may want to consider switching from a system where email news is an option to where it is the standard.

E-news and electronic marketing are very much on the rise. Charities have long since learned that you don't simply make a PDF of your regular newsletter and put everybody's name in the 'cc' box (although sadly, some still do just that!). E-news requires a very different format from hard copy. Usually there will be brief snippets of news and links to your website for those who want more detail. It should also have a link to the *'Donate Now'* page on your website. This is another area where you will almost certainly need some outside help to set up news templates or even host the whole e-news dissemination for you. There are plenty of providers available now and it is not expensive. The savings over printing and postage should cover the cost of outsourcing this activity very quickly indeed.

Social networking is another way of staying in touch with supporters, particularly the younger generations, but increasingly with the older ones too. I am not ashamed to be a 1950s 'baby-boomer' who is addicted to Facebook!

I was recently studying some graphs on donor statistics and noted a surprising jump in the number of 16-24-year-olds who said they had given to charity during the first couple of months of 2010. Could this be because the Red Cross and other leading aid agencies reported their up-to-the-minute relief activities during the Haiti earthquake on Facebook and Twitter? I am sure it was so.

Where to store the data

Your list of friends may well be stored on an Excel spreadsheet or Access database – or even on a card index. Eventually though, as your membership grows, this will not serve you well at all. You will need dedicated fundraising software. There are some excellent packages on the market, some of which are extremely expensive, but increasingly there are more economical systems available. You should be looking for something that will:

• Store the names and addresses of your supporters
• Record when donations are made and the amounts given
• Automatically collect Gift Aid on qualifying donations
• Create mailing and store mailing history
• Create management reports on how a campaign has performed in terms of costs and return on investment.

An excellent little booklet called *'Fundraising Databases: An Introduction to the Setup and Use'* by Peter Flory is available from the Directory of Social Change.[2] You might also ask around some of your fellow charity managers to see what system they are using and how they feel about their choice of software. Whatever you do though, remember when you are setting your budget to include enough for adequate staff training and ongoing IT support costs.

But if you don't ask...

Having individual supporters will not lead to increased income automatically; you will always need to ask them to give. Fundraising textbooks are full of research results that identify motives for giving, but one thing is common to all – people give because they are asked to do so. Do not be frightened of asking your supporters for donations. If one of my close friends or a member of my family was in real need, I would be devastated to discover they had not asked me for help. Your donors feel the same way about what you are doing. They are passionate about your cause, too. Keep them informed of your needs and report back regularly about how your project is going.

Gift Aid – it's a *real gift!*

I cannot understand why so few charities fail to grab the money that the

Government is offering them with open hands – Gift Aid. Put simply, HMRC will pass back to any registered charity the tax (at basic rate) that your donors have already paid on any money they have given to you during the past four years.

Experience has shown that with some effort, 50% of all UK-sourced donations can be accompanied by Gift Aid declarations. A much higher percentage could be eligible but few charities achieve higher than this rate. Steps can be taken to maximise the number of people making Gift Aid declarations by:

- ensuring you have a policy in place for providing a Gift Aid declaration with every donation
- writing to, or telephoning every donor who makes a donation without the declaration, asking if they would be willing to make a Gift Aid declaration
- purchasing fundraising software, as mentioned before, to process Gift Aid claims automatically.

It is also worthwhile informing your supporters who might be paying tax at the higher rate, that they can reclaim the difference between the basic rate of tax on which Gift Aid is based and the higher rate which they have paid. Those who pay the higher rate of tax and who do not complete an annual self-assessment are probably unaware of this. HMRC makes frequent, unannounced audits to small charities to ensure that Gift Aid is not being abused. It is vital to keep an audit trail of all donations received, and original copies of Gift Aid declaration forms should normally be kept for at least 6 years.

Payroll giving – a lost cause?

The Government has invested lots of money and much effort trying to promote *Payroll Giving*, or *Give-As-You-Earn* as it used to be called. Payroll Giving donations are deducted before tax so each £1 given will only cost the donor 80p, or if they are a higher rate tax payer it will only cost 60p. Employees can choose to support any charity of their choice with a regular donation direct from their pay.

My advice? Don't bother – this is a total waste of time unless you are in partnership with a large company that has persuaded a significant number of their employees to join the scheme. The whole process has to be administered by an approved Payroll Giving Agent (who takes a cut) and despite claims that it is easy and simple to set up, relatively few charities have found it beneficial. It's certainly not led to long-term relationship with donors. You would be much better off trying to secure Gift Aid donations directly from the employees because you would then receive the amount donated *plus* the tax relief.

As Ken Burnett, author, lecturer and fellow fundraising consultant, says *'Fundraising is not about money. It's about necessary work that urgently needs doing. It's not about asking people to give – it's about inspiring them to give. The money is just a means to an end.'* [3]

The end is seeing lives changed. It is about hope being restored. It is about communities revitalised and creativity released. Do not become so bogged down in finding the funding that you lose sight of the end result. But never forget that without the funding, you may never achieve the end result.

1 Clarke and Norton, (1997) p.324.
2 www.dsc.org.uk Peter Flory is one of the sector's leading authorities on fundraising databases and has written several excellent books on the subject.
3 Burnett (1996).

Finding more funds

'Fundraising is all about selling an idea to someone who has the means to make it happen.'
Michael Norton

We have just looked at the most important part of your 'income mix' – your individual donors. But now we must spend a moment considering the other options available to you for fundraising. Again, I am not giving you a comprehensive guide here on any of these issues. I am just trying to outline the general principles. Before embarking on any of the following fundraising methods you should really spend some time getting a little training in these areas. There are several one or two-day courses available from a variety of providers, which ought not to break the bank.

Grant-making trusts

It is estimated that there are a total of over 8,000 trusts and foundations in the UK, who annually give £2.7 billion to charitable causes.[1] These trusts and foundations range from some large, very wealthy institutions which are funded by the profits from successful businesses, down to small family trusts who give away the interest from endowments left by a wealthy member of the family.

Applying for a grant from one of these trusts can be very time consuming, and unless you get it right first time, can be very disappointing when your application is rejected. It is quite a specialist task, and if you have never written grant applications before, it is well worth going on a short course in order to learn the 'trade secrets'. The amount you have to pay for training in this area will be repaid many times over once you become successful.

Do your research well

The key to writing grant applications is research. Most applications that fail do so because the request is inappropriate. Asking the wrong trust for the wrong cause is a waste of your time and theirs. Let's say that you are looking for sponsors for a *'Battle of the Bands'* competition to promote young, unsigned rock bands in the London Boroughs of Newham and Tower Hamlets. The fictitious *Ebenezer Smith Foundation* is not likely to give favourable consideration to your application even though you found this trust from a database search for 'London' 'young people' 'arts' and 'music'. Careful reading of their trust criteria will show that they were set up to provide bursaries for young classical musicians who are studying at the Royal College of Music.

So make sure that you spend time finding out exactly what each trust will or will not support. Many trusts publish guidelines on their own websites, or you can find these in one of the directories now available in hard copy or via subscription online.[2] You will need to check if the beneficial area matches where you are working. Some trusts have a specific interest in local work, and while your cause may be exactly what they are interested in, their guidelines might exclude anyone who is not working within a specific regional boundary.

Remember this about trusts; they only exist for one reason, and that is to give money away to good causes like yours. So do not be shy about helping them to do just that!

Government agencies

Both local and central government have funds set aside to help the voluntary sector deliver much-needed services. Much of the grant-making responsibility is no longer carried out directly by government offices, but has been delegated to quangos such as the Arts Council for England or the Countryside Commission. Local government is under increasing pressure these days and much of their spending power has been cut, but if you are providing a service that they would have to deliver if you were not around, you may find that you qualify for assistance with both revenue and capital projects.

Do beware of the contractual nature of statutory grants. They can only be used for the delivery of services that meet the criteria of the government department concerned. It is easy to get into strategic drift here. There could be a temptation to widen the scope of your services just in order to qualify for the grant. Imagine that you are running a local youth club, and are keen to find funding for an arts and drama workshop. You discover that your local County Council is offering a grant for exactly this type of work. But the small-print states that 'all projects must show benefits for ethnic minorities or promote multi-faith involvement' in order to be successful. You could easily find yourselves re-writing the project description to include youngsters from cross-communities and other faith groups, even though you have absolutely no experience in working in these areas, and it was not what you set out to do in the first place. This is very risky and should be avoided at all costs, otherwise your organisation could quickly drift away from meeting its original objectives.

As with grant-making trusts, research is paramount, and it can easily take up much of your time, with no guarantee of results at the end. The Directory of Social Change publishes a *Central Government Grants Guide* which could be a good starting point. You can also subscribe to regular email updates from www.governmentfunding.org.uk which is also run by DSC.

The corporate sector

Historically, many large companies have made donations to charity from their pre-tax profits, and thus reduced their corporation tax liability. Businesses or manufacturing industries often had a vested interest in the local community, for example because they employed many of the local residents or where the local community depended on the industry for economic viability.

In recent times, companies are more prone to give 'gifts in kind' or allow their employees time off to work as volunteers in local charities rather than give outright cash grants. A quick glance at the Corporate Social Responsibility pages on a typical company website might give you the impression that businesses are falling over themselves to help the local community, or international and environmental causes. Without wanting to sound cynical, there is often a certain amount of 'greenwash' in CSR policies. Persuading corporates to part with real cash, unless there is a clear benefit for the company, is very difficult. To be fair to them, they have responsibility to their shareholders to deliver a profit, and helping your cause may not be one of their priorities.

If you are a small charity, you may well find a local business that will be willing to sponsor a fundraising event, either by donating prizes for a draw or by underwriting publicity costs in return for some profiling of their business. A local taxi firm or a family run clothing store that's been on your High Street for several generations may be pleased to make a contribution in return for having their name on your publicity material. Just walk in and ask to speak to the manager. It is a cheap form of advertising for them, and well worth pursuing. Be aware of the grey area of entering into 'trading' when offering advertising space to businesses, if this is not permitted in your trust deed.

Trading activities

Unless your trust deeds specifically allow you do so, you should be cautious about engaging in any substantial trading activity. Technically, 'selling' advertising space in event brochures or other publicity material is 'trading' and in the past has not been approved by the Charity Commission. Its rationale was that the selling of advertising space is not one of your charitable objects. However, it has recently published a more pragmatic opinion on this very matter. Charity law now permits charities to carry on non-primary purpose trading in order to raise funds, provided that the trading involves no significant risk to the assets of the charity.

Primary and non-primary purpose

'Non-primary purpose' means that it has nothing to do with your primary objectives. Let's imagine that your charity supports a group of women in a developing country and you are committed to helping them climb out of the slave-trade of the sex industry. They are involved in the production of women's clothing as part of vocational training, so you could sell that produce and it would be 'primary purpose trading'. On the other hand, a local wildlife conservation charity that is selling Christmas cards is conducting 'non-primary purpose trading', but is allowed to do so because it is not a high risk activity. If you were to produce thousands of expensive calendars which were still not sold by the end of February, it would be 'high risk', and should not be considered.

Incorporation – forming a Trading Company

Most charities that engage in trading (such as running charity shops or selling any form of merchandise to promote the charity) are *incorporated*. That is, they form a *trading company* which donates all its profits back to the charity and thus avoids paying corporation tax. There could be considerable benefit from creating a trading subsidiary in order to maximise income generation.

A trading subsidiary is a company, owned and controlled by one or more charities set up in order to trade. Trading subsidiaries must be used for non-primary purpose trades involving any significant risk.

Charities which want a corporate structure have hitherto had to register both as charities and as companies, which means they had to meet the dual regulatory burdens of both the Charity Commission and Companies House. The Charities Act 2006 created a new vehicle for these charities – the *Charitable Incorporated Organisation* (CIO). A CIO has the advantages of a corporate structure, such as reduced personal liability for trustees, without the burden of dual regulation.[3]

Charity shops

During the recession of 2009-10, charity shops did very well. Fewer people were discarding good clothing than before, but this was made up for by the fact that it became quite 'trendy' to shop in second-hand clothes outlets. There are very real risks of costs exceeding income, but if the shop is staffed by properly trained volunteers, and virtually rent-free premises are obtained, this can prove to be an excellent source of extra income, as well as raising the profile of a charity in the local area. Some charities have found a lucrative market in second-hand furniture. It goes without saying that it is important that any such project is well managed by someone with retail experience.

An alternative to operating a high street shop is to sell items on eBay, which now has a dedicated subsidiary that raises millions of pounds for charity partners.[4]

Counting the real cost

Before leaving these chapters on fundraising, we must give some attention to the cost of fundraising. This is especially important when organising events. Fundraising events are, of course, important for raising income, but are also significant for increasing your organisation's profile and adding names of potential supporters to the database. However, care must be taken when planning any event to ensure that the costs are kept in proportion to the income expected, or as the accountants call it, the '*Return on Investment*' (ROI) – how much we get back for the money we put in. Some fundraisers wrongly assume that as long as they make a profit, all is well. I remember to my embarrassment that I made this mistake many years ago when I was new to event planning and was happy that my anniversary concert had more than broken even on costs. I could not understand why our accountant was so upset that I had spent £3,800 to host an event that raised £4,200 on the night. The reason he was so concerned was that the Charity Commission expects you to spend most of your donated money on your beneficiaries, achieving an approved charitable purpose. 'Fundraising' is not one of their thirteen approved charitable purposes.[5]

The Charity Commission will be looking at all fundraising costs as a percentage of the income gained. There are no fixed rules, but a good guideline is that an event should never cost more than 33% of the expected income, (which is an ROI ratio of 2:1).

Left singing for your supper

When organising events that have high set-up costs, such as dinners or concerts, you will need to be able to show that sufficient new donors are gained from this one event to justify the initial costs, by spreading the Return on Investment over the expected *lifetime value* (LTV) of the new donors.

Let me illustrate this:

Supposing you held a charity dinner that cost in total £5,000 to host. Ticket sales for the dinner, raffle tickets and an 'auction of promises' at the event brought in a total of £6,000. Your auditors would not be too excited about this as an acceptable ROI. But if you were able to demonstrate to your auditor that all the tickets sold, and the bids at the auction brought in 300 new names and addresses that could be used for 'prospect mailing', which, over a period of the next five years, might be expected to generate £10,000 for the charity, the event would be considered worthwhile. *Return on Investment* should always take into consideration the lifetime value of any assets gained, not just the immediate return.

Charities in Scotland are now required by OSCR to complete a *Supplementary Monitoring Return* each year, in which they are required to state specifically the cost of generating all funds compared to the amount raised. Both OSCR and the Charity Commission are getting tough on this. Failure to satisfy them with your Annual Report could provoke an unwanted inspection or audit of your activities. Ultimately they could close your organisation down if they were not convinced that you were using donors' money wisely.

I would recommend avoiding 'high risk' activities such as outdoor events, where bad weather might keep the crowds away, or events such as concerts that involve high set-up costs. You can insure against wet weather spoiling your event. I did this once, but the premium was horrendous – we could probably have found better odds with a local bookie!

Telephone madness

I once did an audit of an international charity that was spending a huge amount of donated income on a telephone campaign with an agency that was bringing in only a 20% profit margin. I explained to the executive that the money spent on hiring the agency would be more likely to bring in a higher ROI if invested in a direct mail campaign or other prospecting activity. In doing this, their trustees had unwittingly become guilty of not using their charity's funds in the best interest of the charity.

You could be surprised, after a little research, how many different sources of funds there are available to you. If it sounds a bit daunting to go after them – it needn't be. With some careful planning, now that you are aware of the pitfalls, these funds can be realistically tapped. Trusts and grants are there to be used. You may also find you can run an event that makes a respectable profit. And events can also generate lots of *fun* along with the *funds!*

1 According to the Association of Charitable Foundations.

2 The most commonly used directory is Grant Making Trusts produced by the Directory of Social Change, available in an online format as well as in hard copy.

3 At the time of writing this book, legislation to introduce CIOs has still not been finalised, but it is expected to be completed in mid-2011.

4 See www.missionfish.org

5 See www.charity-commission.gov.uk – Guidance on Charitable Purposes. In reality, this particular event could not be measured as straightforward costs versus income. It was as much about raising the charity profile as fundraising, and also brought in many new donors whose lifetime value pushed the ROI beyond the next 5 years. But I have included it here as an illustration of how ignorance can be a dangerous bliss in fundraising!

Developing donors

'There is no such thing as donor fatigue; the public think small charities are great.'
Joe Saxton

Up until now you will have probably focused most of your attention on the people who will be on the receiving end of the charity work, your beneficiaries. It is vital that you keep focused on them and their needs. But, as we have already said, the other group that you must keep in mind are the supporters and donors, without whom you will not be able to meet the needs of the beneficiaries. Again, it's all about keeping the Triangle in proportion.

Some of these people will prove to be just as passionate about your cause as you are; many of them will be giving generously and sometimes sacrificially to your work. They deserve to be treated as more than just a name or number on a database. You need to start regarding them as your closest friends.

Build lasting relationships

Think about your own close friends for a moment. You keep in touch with them either by letter or, more often these days, by email and Facebook. You call them on the phone. You remember their birthdays, and you share in their joys and sorrows. You keep a record of their address and other details, probably on an electronic contact list on your computer or phone. You make sure the list is kept up to date, for fear of losing contact with your friends.

In a true friendship, you don't just communicate to them about your own needs and latest news; you will want to listen to *their* needs and hear about what they have been doing too. When they send you a gift, you immediately call them to thank them, not just because you don't want to offend them, but because you are genuinely pleased. If you lose contact with them for any length of time, you assume that they no longer value your friendship as much as they once did, and the relationship starts to drift apart.

All of the above ought to apply equally to your 'friends' who are your supporters. Some organisations go as far to refer to their supporters as 'Friends of St Mary's Hospice' or whatever your charity is called. However, your supporters cannot be just 'friends' in name only. You must treat them as friends if you want to maintain the relationship. The more you communicate with them, especially if you allow them to choose the preferred mode of communication, the more you will be able to develop the relationship.

I said earlier that I would recommend some good fundraising materials as we go along. One of the best books written on the subject is *Relationship Fundraising* by Ken Burnett. This book is definitely the industry benchmark on creating friendships that lead to funds. When you have read that, you might want to try one of his other books, *Friends for Life*.

So who are your friends?

As the list of your supporters grows, you will need to manage the acquisition and maintenance of supporters very carefully. In Chapter 5, we spoke about the necessity of investing in a robust database in order to manage the data you have for each of your supporters. Make it easier for yourself by collecting enough information about your supporters *at the point of acquisition*. There are some basic essentials that you must get, such as name and address (including Postcode) and phone number, but also important these days is an email address and mobile phone number. But have you considered how helpful it is to know the gender of the person who has signed up to your mailing list? With the cultural diversity that now exists in this country, it is often impossible to know whether you should be writing to a 'Mr' or 'Mrs', let alone a 'Ms'.

Welcome

Some organisations make the mistake of adding all new contacts directly on to their main mailing list. The worst thing that could happen to a new 'friend' is to receive a direct mail appeal as their first piece of communication from you. You should develop a policy whereby each new supporter, however they have been acquired, receives a 'welcome pack' as soon as possible after the first contact is made. They may have sent in a gift, in which case a personal 'thank you' should be included in the pack, but even if they have just asked to be included in future mailings, the welcome pack should express appreciation for that too. The pack might also include a short questionnaire asking them for more information about themselves *'in order that we might be able to send you appropriate information which will be of interest to you'.*

That extra information might be:

- Age band; you can even get away with asking for date of birth these days
- Email address, if not already given
- Preferred means of communication (mail through the post or email)
- Permission to make occasional phone calls – if so please give daytime phone number and/or mobile number
- What particular aspect of the charity's work are they especially interested in (maybe it will be child sponsorship, healthcare, HIV support, etc)
- Some charities find it helpful to know the marital status of their supporters too, but initially you do not want to be too intrusive.[1]

It's good to talk

Direct mail is still a very effective form of communicating with your supporters, but it is becoming increasingly expensive and the returns on investment are beginning to decline as the general public are cautious about so called 'junk mail'. Junk mail is only the wrong mail sent to the wrong person at the wrong time. Carefully targeted mailings that are in keeping with what the supporter has requested, and containing information that is relevant to the supporter, will never be junk mail.

I would be very unlikely to respond to a cold mailing (no name and address, delivered by Royal Mail to every household) on behalf of a breast cancer charity. I might open the envelope to retrieve the free pen though. But had my daughter opened the envelope it might have been a different matter. One of her best friends died of breast cancer recently. On the other hand, I did respond to a cold mailing from the Royal British Legion once. I knew the guy in the story that popped uninvited through my letterbox – we had been paratroopers together – and I remembered that he was badly wounded during the Falklands War. One person's junk mail might be just the right thing for someone else, which is why it still widely used.

Do not make the mistake of trying to copy direct mail programmes used by the larger charities. You may think that because their mailshot brings in thousands of pounds, all you need to do is copy their format and it will work for you – it won't. But if you only have a few hundred supporters, you have one huge advantage over Oxfam or Save the Children – you can genuinely personalise many of your letters. Go through your mailing list and segment all the people you know personally. You should hand-write the salutation and sign each of these letters. These are your friends – treat them as such. Take advantage of being small, because (hopefully, now that you are reading this) it won't last for ever.

Growing and nurturing

Your charity needs to develop relationships with supporters who are not yet active donors, and encourage them to make their first and second gifts. This is called *donor development*. (By the way, I wish the voluntary sector could come up with a better term than 'donors' – to me 'donors' give blood and other vital organs! Isn't there a more appropriate, warmer description for someone who invests in a cause they are fervent about?)

Donor development is not about manipulating people; it is about investing in relationships because you care about them. It is important to understand that the relationship with supporters cannot just be left to chance. Enquirers do not suddenly become first-time donors without some stimulus. Committed donors will not usually leave legacies unless they are asked to do so.

The key ingredients in donor development are:

- communication
- engagement
- appreciation

The need to *communicate* regularly and appropriately with donors is probably already important to you. There is also a need to *engage* donors with the cause. Invite them to get involved in the operational process, not just to attend fundraising events. Ask supporters for their views and ideas. In general, make them feel as if they own the cause. In this way they will become 'stakeholders' and not just 'data'.

We have already said that showing *appreciation* is much more than just good manners. A personal, friendly 'thank you' letter may not make economical sense for every £5 gift received, but taking a longer view, the elderly gentleman who gave up a portion of his pension to make that gift deserves to be treated with respect. He may also be considering leaving a legacy to you. The young girl who sends in £3 from her pocket money or cake bake project may be working in one of your orphanages overseas one day. *It has also been known for major donors to test the reaction they receive by giving a small donation before making a substantial gift!*

Not left standing

Some charities are very good about thanking one-off donors for each gift, or subsequent gifts, but then forget to thank their supporters who give by standing order. This means that they are treating their 'casual' supporters far better than they are treating their most loyal friends. A 'thank you' letter should be sent at least once a year to all supporters who give by standing order. And don't forget those who have given online – especially if they are a first-time donor who is simply supporting a friend taking part in a 10k run for your charity. Yes, they will have received an automatic response to their gift, but a more personal note or email might well seal a future relationship with them.

Last year, I undertook a major challenge event for a cause I feel really strongly about. I raised over £1,500 from friends and family, most of it online. The charity concerned wrote and thanked me politely for the two small cheques I sent in through the post, but they ignored the amount I had raised online. I was disappointed in them from a professional point of view, but I have to admit I was also hurt personally.

Next to your fundraising appeals, your donation 'thank you' letter is the most important communication that a donor receives. So it ought to sparkle with sincerity and not appear as a mass produced monologue beginning 'Dear Supporting Friend...' I don't write to any of my real friends that way, do you?

The Donor Pyramid

You don't have to have been around fundraisers for very long before you will hear someone referring to the '*Donor Pyramid*' (Figure 2). No, it's not about Tutankhamun's legacy to the British Museum – it is a simple model borrowed from commercial marketing that illustrates the ultimate direction that any donor development strategy should take. It draws donors into a deepening relationship with the organisation and then gradually moves them on to the next stage of their support, loyalty and understanding.

It's exactly the same as any developing relationship really – boy meets girl at night club; he invites her on a date; she thinks it might be cool so accepts.

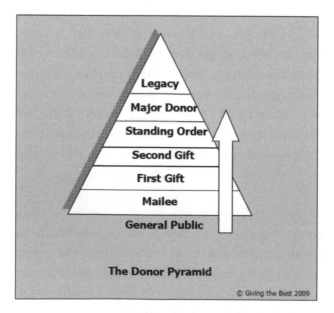

Figure 2

After the second date, they both think there is some chemistry developing and they become 'an item'. A few months later, they are engaged, married, and eventually they are raising a family of their own. We all recognise the process, but we also know it doesn't happen without some constructive action being taken by both partners. It is the same with donors. They will not become best friends unless you are proactive.

Some textbooks would prefer to display the pyramid inverted, since the value of a legacy usually outweighs the total lifetime giving of most donors. But the reality is that as donors progress on their journey/relationship with an organisation, their numbers inevitably become fewer, ultimately illustrating the Pareto principle: 80% of your income will come from 20% of your donors. I prefer to think of it as a railway line that doesn't really converge; it just appears to do so because of the perspective of distance.

Not all donors will progress all the way to the top of the pyramid. Research has shown that the average donor will stay active with a favourite charity for only 5-6 years. This is particularly true of donors from Generations X and Y (those born during the '70s and '80s) who relish the changing seasons of life and move on to newer causes very quickly. My own father, who was part of the 'Seniors Generation' born in the 1920s, supported the same causes for most of his life and left legacies to two of them. He had progressed all the way to the top of the pyramid, but I happen to know that it was because the two organisations concerned encouraged him to do so.

The most important question which every charity ought to ask about the Pyramid is 'are we investing at the right level?' It is too easy to spend most of the fundraising budget on the lower levels, trying to get the first gift, while ignoring the 'gold mine' of major donors and legacies at the top.

Losing friends

Although some donor attrition is inevitable, it is a mistake to just sit back and let it happen. It is frequently said to be ten times more costly to find new donors than it is to keep the ones you've already got. Are you aware of the attrition rate of your supporters? You may be able to tell me how many active donors you have now and how many you had last year, but are they the same people? How many are you losing along the way; does your bucket have too many holes in it?

When I do audits of charities, I always ask the relevant department if they would know if a standing order from a supporter had been cancelled. Many organisations do not have any mechanism to spot this. I discovered this for myself some years ago when I was reviewing my charity giving and I cancelled a substantial standing order that I had made to a charity for over ten years. With a slight amount of 'professional intrigue', I then sat back and waited to see what happened. Nothing! They didn't notice. Not even a letter to say 'We are sorry to see you go...'! Our gas, electricity or phone companies do much better than that when we switch providers!

There could be many reasons why a standing order has been cancelled. It could well be a bank error, and the money that was intended for you may be going into someone else's account. You may have unwittingly offended the donor, or they may have fallen on hard times and had to cut back on their giving. Pick up the phone. Explain to the donor that you have noticed that their payments have stopped and you just want to confirm that this was intentional. Then ask, politely, if they were offended or disappointed by anything you have done and seek to address any concerns they might have. If they have just been made redundant or facing other financial hardship, express your concern and your gratitude for the support they have given and ask if you can still continue to send them news from time to time. Keep the relationship open whatever it takes. Don't write them off just because they have stopped giving.

Best friends

We have already touched briefly on the subject of '*High-Value Donors*' (HVDs) – sometimes referred to as *Major Donors*. There are different definitions of what makes someone a High-Value Donor, but the one most generally used is someone who has given in excess of £1,000 in a single gift, usually during the past 3 years. It may have been a one-off gift as a result of a lottery win or a legacy bequest, but generally, people who have given £1,000 or more have the propensity to give much more than that. You should not be embarrassed about asking them to do just that. But remember that this group of people will not respond to direct mail shots; you need to go and ask them face-to-face. The easy part of the process is that played by the donor. Writing a four-figure cheque for charity is something which many wealthy people do quite regularly. The challenging part is in identifying suitable prospects and making 'the ask' in an appropriate manner.

Fundraising from HVDs is often overlooked as being too challenging a task, but it is one of the most cost-effective methods of fundraising available. The workload involved in identifying and nurturing just a handful of individuals is much less than it takes to raise the same amount of income through direct mailings. Make sure you include this in your fundraising strategy, and get some training for yourself or one of your team on how to do it.

Segmentation

Mention has already been made of the need to collect and manage details about your supporters so that you can communicate with them more effectively. If you already have a database or list of names and addresses but know very little else about them, it is worth sending out a simple questionnaire to build up a better picture of who your donors are. You can employ a market research company to do this for you, but it is very expensive, so unless you have many thousands of donors already, I would steer well clear of that for now. Knowing the age bracket of your donors, their giving history, their interests and preferences will allow you to '*segment*' your database. This means dividing the data up into mailing groups. So for instance, you do not want to be sending an appeal letter to someone who is already giving to you by standing order each month. That just sends the message that you are taking them for granted. Instead, they should get a letter with news and updates about how their contribution is making a difference to your work. Periodically, you might like to ask them to consider increasing the amount they are giving.

When my kids lived at home, I noticed that one of my daughters, who was supporting the same charity as me, received a different mailing than the one I had received. They had segmented their mailing based on age profile, and she received something much more upbeat and youth orientated than the one I received – actually, I preferred the one she received!

History is important

Segmentation is also important when it comes to giving history. You should be prepared to mail those who have given regularly much more often than those who have never given. It's a basic marketing principle. Analyse your mailing list and mail only to the top 90% of responders. Don't cut off the non-responders, but don't spend a lot of money sending them quarterly appeals that don't work. Maybe once a year will be enough to keep them 'warm'.

This is where you may need some outside help with setting up your database. I know charities that have bought the most expensive brand-leader fundraising software and only use it for printing address labels. Groan! Investing in help for some simple segmentation and campaign analysis will pay dividends many times over. The Institute of Fundraising website has a Directory of Consultants where you can search for help with database management.[2]

We really do care

We have been talking in this chapter about building and developing relationships. Later on we will be talking about the different personalities it takes to build an effective team. You will need to think seriously about who on your team is going to handle 'supporter relations' issues. As well as being confident with handling data they will also need to have excellent 'people skills' too. Imagine that 'Doris Donor from Dorchester', who has received regular letters from your National Director addressed to 'Dear Doris', phones up to tell you her cat has died. This is devastating for her. She is looking for a listening ear from her 'friends'. Friendship has to be a two-way relationship. You need to be interested in 'Doris' herself, not just her money.

Donors quickly recognise if they are being used or manipulated. On the other hand, they will appreciate organisations that demonstrate that they care about their stakeholders.

Getting personal

When my father died a few years ago, I had the task of phoning round to the many charities he supported to ask them to remove his name from their mailing list. The first one I called put me through to the accounts department – they had no dedicated supporter relations person it would appear – and I had obviously interrupted an accountant or bookkeeper immersed in their spreadsheets. They were only interested in doing just what I asked, locating my father's record on the screen and marking it as 'deceased'. 'How do you spell his name? What is the Postcode...?' No compassion as to the fact that I was grieving or recognition that my father had supported this cause generously for many years. My opinion of that otherwise brilliant organisation went rapidly downhill. In contrast, a few minutes later I received a call from a salesman who had been trying to sell my father a stair lift. When I told him my father had just died, he could have just rung off – he wasn't going to make his sale after all. But instead, he spoke to me for several minutes about Dad. What a contrast in relational marketing! (I know where to go if I ever need a stair lift!)

Donors are 'family friends'

So, we need to be careful how we communicate with donors. They are best friends. They are family. You may eventually decide to employ a dedicated member of staff to handle communications. Such a person would still sit in the bottom left hand corner of the Triangle, because it is still a function of resourcing.

One thing you must never forget, though, is that 'supporter relationships', as with any PR, is the responsibility of everyone in the organisation. The big corporate organisations spend millions of pounds creating a *corporate identity* that we will instantly recognise through logos and house colours. But some of them, especially banks, airlines, and fast-food chains forget that the most junior employee will be the one who creates (or destroys) the *corporate image*.

Counter culture

I changed my bank a few years ago because I could not tolerate the poor counter service I was getting at my previous one. A check-in clerk was rude to me once at Heathrow and it was several years before I could bring myself to fly on that airline again. It is the same with charities. All your staff need to be aware that they create a positive or negative image of your work every time they engage with the general public. How will you help them to turn that into one of your strengths?

We have been round the Triangle and looked in some detail now at three of the four Critical Success Factors. The one we have not looked at is *Service Delivery* – I hope you are not disappointed, but we are not going there. As I have already said, service delivery is probably something you are already pretty good at, and it is unlikely that I can add to the skills you already have. Instead, we are now going to spend time digging deeper into the 'dark myths' of *strategic planning*. Don't worry – we are going to take it very slowly.

---

1 Data protection laws only allow you to store information about your supporters that is relevant to their relationship with you.

2 www.institute-of-fundraising.org.uk/consultants

8 Planning on a Purpose

'You've got to be very careful if you don't know where you're going, because you might not get there.'
Lawrence P Berra

You really *do* need to have a dream to follow – but then make plans to get there. Some people always live in a dream world, and there are others who like to face reality; and then there are those who turn the one into the other. *These* are the people who understand the strategic process. This chapter will help clarify the process so that it becomes as natural as getting dressed in the morning.

Structure and Strategy

I hope that by now you are getting the picture. *Structure* – the right people doing the right jobs and in the right relationship to each other – is as important as the *strategy* which, as we have already said, is about the 'big picture', the 'long view'. It is about knowing where the eventual destination will be so that you can make detours to overcome obstacles, without getting completely lost en route.

Kenneth Mackenzie is considered by many to be a leading guru on organisational structures. He teaches that the *structure* must follow the *strategy*. In other words, first decide what you want to do, then build an organisation to deliver the goods.[1] That's fine for multi-national corporations, but for the emerging voluntary organisation like yours, you probably have to work with what you've got – and that maybe you, the dog, and a friend who comes in part-time to stuff the newsletters into envelopes.

However, without having even the basics of a strategic plan, you will quickly get bogged down with the day-to-day issues, some of which might be leading you in completely the wrong direction. We will look in more detail about creating a strategic plan in Chapter 10. For now, I want to talk about basic principles – the groundwork. I am going to help you prepare the trenches into which you will later plant your seed potatoes.

I am often asked to help prepare fundraising plans for capital projects. My initial question is usually something along the lines of *'Where does this project fit in your strategic plan?'* And I get a blank or defensive reply. All too often, the project in question has not been born out of strategic thinking but *'a trustee thought it was a good idea at the time'*. Sometimes the project does not even help the charity to achieve its charitable objects at all!

Focus on the real goal

One of my very first clients, a creative arts charity for young people, told me with great excitement that the property next door to them had suddenly come on the market and they wanted to raise funds to purchase it. Their 'vision' was for it to be converted for use as a rehab centre for drug and substance abusers. Great idea; great opportunity! The trouble was that this activity, however socially commendable, was totally outside their approved charitable objects. Had the trustees looked at this strategically, they would have realized that they were being diverted from the original plan by a 'pop-up' opportunity. Actually, I find that many small charities simply do not have a strategic plan at all. Others might have had one but it stayed in the filing cabinet and bore no resemblance to the actual work accomplished. It was simply a paper exercise that ticked the right boxes at the time in order to get registered.

It is not just new charities that lose the plot on strategy. I come across many well-established organisations that are experiencing this kind of *'strategic drift'*. Professor Roger Courtney describes it thus:

'Around the original core of uniqueness, encrustations are added incrementally. Like barnacles, these need to be removed to reveal the underlying strategic positioning.'[2]

These organisations really need to rediscover their original strategic priorities and get back to doing what they do best. In the case of the creative arts group, it was obvious to me that the founders had gathered around themselves one or two friends to be trustees in order to satisfy the minimum legal requirement of the charity registration. I am quite sure that these friends fully supported the aims and ideals of the organisation, but I doubt if they had fully grasped the responsibilities and requirements of Governance. But the Charity Commissioners can be pretty firm in these cases.

In February 2010, the Charity Commission told an Islamic relief charity that its plans to build a 5,000-pupil boarding school for Muslim girls were not within its objects, and they were forced to return all the money they had raised for the project. There was nothing wrong in building a school for Muslim girls – it was that they were the wrong people to be doing it because their stated object was 'the relief of financial hardship caused by famine, war or other disaster in any part of the world' not 'providing education'.

Strategy unpacked

Strategic planning need not be complicated. Anyone who has had teenagers will recognise these two scenarios:

Jack: 'Dad, can you lend me fifty quid?'
Dad: 'Why do you need fifty quid?'
Jack: 'I need some new trainers.'
Dad: 'What is wrong with the ones you are wearing?'
Jack: 'Aw, Dad, they are so non-cool now. I need a pair like the other guys are wearing, you know...'

Dad *doesn't* know, actually! And Jack has not planned his strategy, and is probably not going to get his dream Nike Air Max this way. By comparison, his cousin Tanya has a much better approach.

Tanya: 'Dad, thank you for coming to pick me up last night. I felt awful to have to call you so late, but none of the guys had cars, and I knew how you hate me to be out so late on my own.'
Dad: 'That's what Dads are for, Tan; you know I'd do anything for my little girl!'
Tanya: 'Yeah, I know...' (She gives him a hug and he responds with a knowing smile). 'Dad, I noticed that New Look has a sale on right now, and

there's this winter jacket I really love, and my green one is getting so tatty and probably won't last until next winter…but I can't afford it this month. I was wondering if you could lend me £50 so I can get it now and save around £25 on the normal price? I am working an extra shift on Friday nights so will be able to pay you back in a couple of weeks!'

It is not that Tanya's father is a soft touch, but she is much more likely to succeed in her fundraising project because she has planned her strategy well. She builds upon a relationship; she has presented a strong case for support; she has presented a budget plan and demonstrated that the loan is a safe investment. Her father will probably come up with the loan, even though he suspects that it will actually be much longer than a couple of weeks before he sees the £50 again.

In the same way, planning strategically is vital for each of the three core activities (CSFs) of the Triangle of Sustainability.

• Those who are at the sharp end, responsible for *service delivery*, need a strategic plan so that they can concentrate on the immediate needs of those they are trying to help.

• *Trustees* need to set strategic direction so that the charity can move forward to achieve the agreed objectives.

• Those who are *fundraising* need to be aware of these plans, and prepare their own strategy for generating the income needed to resource these projects and activities.

It's actually all one plan, but with three elements that make up the whole. But you can understand that it must all be going in the same direction.

The process
The strategic process is very much rooted in your *Purpose* and *Vision* statements. Again, I am using expressions that you will often find in management seminars or books. I have tried to explain them in everyday

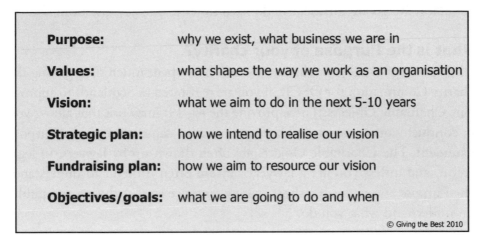

Purpose:	why we exist, what business we are in
Values:	what shapes the way we work as an organisation
Vision:	what we aim to do in the next 5-10 years
Strategic plan:	how we intend to realise our vision
Fundraising plan:	how we aim to resource our vision
Objectives/goals:	what we are going to do and when

© Giving the Best 2010

Figure 3 – The Strategic Process

language so that you will not be afraid of using them – and understand what you are talking about.

Figure 3 shows the relationship between the six key statements that enable strategy to cascade down from one layer to the next. Each level becomes more specific and provides the means of achieving the level above. *Purpose, Values* and *Vision* are long term, visionary and idealistic, but they need some more specific plans in order for the 'ideals' to become reality.

It is beyond the scope of this book to go into great depth on the process of strategic planning. There are many books and courses available on the subject. But every leader of any organisation that is working in the voluntary sector needs to learn how to think *strategically* before they can begin the all-important task of raising funds to support the work of the organisation. All too often you probably find yourself in survival mode; just coping with today or at best, the next few days' tasks. Take some time out, maybe away from the office or wherever you work, and try to think about the longer-term issues. Asking donors to support your work is like going to your bank manager for a business loan; you need to convince them that you know what you are about, where you want to go, and how you intend to go about it, before they will entrust you with their money.

But before we go any further, we do need to settle one key question:

What is the Purpose of your charity?

When you registered your charity, you will have spent much time getting the Charity Commission (or OSCR, if you are registered in Scotland) to approve your Charitable Objects. These provide the legal framework that allows you to conduct your activities. They are not the same thing as a Purpose Statement. The Charitable Objects are often drawn up by lawyers, in legal jargon, and unless you are a lawyer, they are often difficult to understand. The Purpose Statement is a short snappy sentence so that the general public can understand what you do.

'Our Purpose is to preserve the ancient art of Japanese flower-arranging.'

or   educate people on planning ahead for dementia

'To provide holidays for disabled children who live in Brighton.'

It is clear and concise. The Purpose Statement must not contradict the Charitable Objects, of course; it just expresses them in language that everyone can understand. Unless a Purpose is clearly articulated throughout the organisation, staff may eventually begin to ask 'What are we really here for?' Without a clear Purpose Statement it is difficult to motivate the members of the organisation.

So, if you haven't got one yet, put it down as the Number One Priority on your 'to do' list. It's vital. If you go to any major donor or trust for funding, they will say *'So, tell me about your organisation. What do you do?'* Give them your Purpose Statement. You know it without even needing to look it up. It's a one-liner. It is exciting and dynamic.

I sometimes practice a little 'role play' at my seminars when I ask delegates to imagine that they find themselves alone in a lift with Richard Branson or Bill Gates. Each delegate has 30 seconds to explain what their organisation does and why the millionaire should make a donation to them. It is very obvious which delegates do not know their own purpose statements!

In the frame

Some organisations use the term *'Mission'* instead of *'Purpose'*, but *'Mission'* can mean different things to different groups, particularly within the context of faith groups. I prefer to use *'Purpose'* as an unequivocal term which describes the organisation's reason for existence. I often see so-called 'Mission Statements' written on school staff room walls, or company websites, which are actually more about Vision than Purpose. They describe an ideal that they would like to achieve rather than their core business. Here is an example I have grabbed at random off the internet from a junior school in Nottinghamshire:

'To make our good better, and our better best.'

It's quite motivational, and inspirational, but it does not describe the core business at all, which is presumably to provide quality education to junior age children in a safe and happy environment. As it stands, the above statement could easily be applied to a local swimming club or micro-brewery! The articulation of your Purpose, if correctly achieved, will communicate clearly and succinctly the what, how, and why of your organisation.

Some different Purpose Statements

Consider these two examples of Purpose Statements from a couple of the UK's best known charities:

'To provide counselling and advice for children and young people in trouble, need or danger by means of free confidential helpline services.' (Childline)

'To end cruelty to children.' (NSPCC)

Both are inspirational and easy to understand, but whereas the first one describes exactly the *what, how, and why* of Childline, the second example simply expresses a dream that is never likely to be achieved. It says nothing of the means that NSPCC uses to meet their objectives. I would not like to work for an organisation that had an unachievable Purpose. It does not motivate me, despite being a passionate and easily remembered little phrase.

Here are some more examples of Purpose Statements that really work:

'To provide guide dogs, mobility and other rehabilitation services that meet the needs of blind and partially sighted people.' (Guide Dogs)

'We exist to champion the rights of everyone with dementia and those who care for them.' (Alzheimer's Society)

'Save the Children fights for children's rights; we deliver immediate and lasting improvement to children's lives worldwide.' (Save the Children)

'Our aim is that disabled people achieve equality: a society in which they are as valued and have the same human and civil rights as everyone else.' (Scope)[3]

Once you have a clear idea about what business you are in and where you want to be going with that business, only then can you begin to set a strategy for achieving those ends. So let's look now at where you want that 'business' to be heading – what your *Vision* is for the future, and what *Values* are going to control how you get there.

---

1 Kenneth D. Mackenzie, (2004).

2 Porter (1997) in Courtney (2002), p.182.

3 Scope is a particularly interesting case study. Originating in 1953 as 'The Spastics Society', it has changed its branding, for obvious reasons, but also broadened its Purpose to include all disabled people, not just those with cerebral palsy.

Values
and Vision

It's about looking ahead

I hope you are beginning to understand that this strategy stuff is not very difficult. *Values* and *Vision* are actually part of our everyday life. We make decisions about what we want to do in the future all the time, and we shape those decisions by what is important to us. So after last year's disastrous camping holiday, you decide that next year you would like to go abroad to somewhere warm, full board, and just lie on a beach, with sun lounger thrown in, but you want to go in June before the schools break up. That's *Vision*. But you also apply your *Values* to it by stipulating that you don't want to be near any expat night clubs, and you don't want to travel too far because you are concerned about your carbon footprint. It's exactly the same for an organisation like yours.

What shapes the way we work as an organisation?

I have chosen to deal with *Values* before we address *Vision* because I believe that the things that are important to us will help us shape where we want to be in the future. Sometimes Values are simplistically described as *'the way we do things around here'*.

According to one leadership training organisation, the Teal Trust,

'Organizational values define the acceptable standards which govern the behaviour of individuals within the organization. Without such values, individuals will pursue behaviours that are in line with their own individual value systems, which may lead to behaviours that the organization doesn't wish to encourage. The organization's values must be in line with its purpose

or mission, and the vision that it is trying to achieve.'[1]

Why values are important

Having a set of clearly defined Values will help protect the integrity of an organisation. They become a benchmark or yardstick against which each new opportunity or partnership can be judged. As such, they can prevent a charity from unwittingly being dragged into an activity which might damage the organisation's moral fibre and public confidence. They are also vitally important to anyone seeking to build partnerships outside of your organisation, whether that is with major donors or on the service delivery side, with someone doing similar work to you. The first thing any potential partner will want to know is *'Does this organisation share our own Values and can we work with them?'* It will be important, then, that your Values are clearly articulated, and are available for public scrutiny, preferably on your website.

Not so easy

It has been my experience that the process of actually writing down Core Values can be one of the hardest elements of the strategic process. You might know in your heart what you hold dear, but can you express it in hard copy? One helpful way to start is to look at a number of organisations which have similar aims to yours and see how they have approached the issue. You will not necessarily want to copy their words or statements, but it can be helpful to see the format they have used in expressing those ideals.

Here is an extract of World Vision's Values:

- *We speak and act honestly. We are open and factual in our dealings with donors, project communities, governments and the public at large.*
- *We demand of ourselves high standards of professional competence and financial accountability.*[2]

In the above illustration, I have underlined words that express passion and high ideals. These words tell me something about the organisation that I need to know if I am interested in partnering with them in any way. Yes, I can work with these guys – they do things my way!

Sorting your Values out

When facilitating sessions with Boards and Management to draw up Values, I usually start with a flip chart and get those present to call out the words that express what they most believe about their organisation.

They usually come up with words such as:

Integrity   Compassion   Diversity   Empowerment   Respect
Teamwork   Trust   Inclusion   Transparency
Accountability   Excellence   Honouring   Developing
Relevant   Dynamic   Innovative   Punctual

This 'brain-storming' session can then lead to drafting of statements which express the ideals of the organisation. But beware! Those involved in the process will be tempted to include their own *personal values*, which are not necessarily the same as *organisational values*. My own personal values have been developed through input from my parents, my faith, my culture, my political beliefs, my individual circumstances, all of which are important to me and help shape the way I behave and react to any given circumstance. But I might be working in an organisation that has been shaped by a different set of cultural ideals, which are equally important but quite different from my own.[3]

There may be times when personal values prevent you from working with an organisation that has widely different organisational values of course. I once turned down work from a sporting and hunting group because my own love of bird-watching and membership of the RSPB was totally at odds with the values of those who paid money to be able to shoot red grouse and partridge for sport.

Practising what you preach

A couple of years ago, I was challenged by the fact that I was teaching these issues in seminars to clients and yet we did not have our own company Core Values on our website. It was an interesting exercise to construct our own Values page. Our company is not a charity but it exists uniquely to serve the voluntary sector, so our Values had to reflect the kinds of ideals one might expect within that sector.

This is part of what we eventually came up with:

'In all our dealings with clients, colleagues, the media and the general public, we act with honesty and transparency. We value financial integrity and accountability. We will not promise what we cannot deliver. By calling the company 'Giving the Best' we have set ourselves a bench mark for excellence and dependability.'[4]

It is particularly important that your Values are not just ticking the right boxes for your corporate image. Roger Courtney, in his book *Strategic Management for Voluntary Nonprofit Organisations*, has underlined this fact:

'There are many organisations with charters or statements of values or beliefs that bear little relationship to how the organisation actually works and deals with customers/clients in practice. This can result in cynicism, both internally and externally.'[5]

Get your Values right... and your donors and service users will value you more!

Working in wonderland

So we now know what business we are in and what will shape the way we work. Now we must decide where we are going. Not knowing where you want to go can leave you in an 'Alice in Wonderland' scenario:

'Cheshire Puss, would you tell me, please, which way I ought to go from here?'
'That depends a good deal on where you want to get to,' said the Cat.
'I don't much care where,' said Alice.
'Then it doesn't matter which way you go,' said the Cat.[6]

What we aim to do in the next 3-5 years

Your Vision statement should clarify where you expect the organisation to be heading; it's all about direction, and therefore must be futuristic in orientation. Unlike Purpose, which as I have already stated, must be realistic, Vision is allowed to be an aspiration. It can be a dream. Some organisations adopt Vision statements that describe the world they are working in and how they would like to see it, eg *'a world where everyone has the same opportunities ... to*

We are passionate about supporting people on their own dementia journey through legal information provision

live in prosperity...' I personally prefer a Vision statement that is more focused on what the organisation itself will be like in the future, because the members of the organisation can see a direct outcome of their Purpose and Values in realising the Vision. So, the previous statement could be tweaked to read *'we will create opportunities for those we serve to achieve prosperity.'* Vision statements are not goals or objectives but, like goals, they need to be couched in measurable terms. I like to see Vision stated as *'what we will become and achieve'* and *'by when'*. So, an example of what that would look like might be:

'By the year 2015, The Sarah Jones Trust will have become an internationally respected agency delivering primary healthcare throughout Southern Africa.'

Sometimes it can be helpful to add a further sentence to qualify and quantify the initial statement:

'This will be evidenced by:
- *a network of 50 clinics in four separate countries*
- *120 fully-trained field workers*
- *an annual turnover of £2 million*
- *a donor base of 20,000 supporters in the UK and beyond.'*

That may be an unrealistic dream, but it is inspirational and measurable. It will give a clear sense of direction to those responsible for operational planning.

In practice, setting the organisational Vision is best achieved by involving as many of the staff as is practically possible. If everyone has had an input into the process, they are much more likely to own the outcome than if a pre-prepared statement is thrust upon them from the founder. For small organisations, the whole staff might be able to get away for a day, but in larger agencies, senior management could take time to hold focus groups with smaller teams of staff, so that their ideas and dreams can be fed into the melting pot that is stirred by a senior management team. It is vital that Jennifer, who works in Accounts, feels that she has had input into this process.

Once you have a clear idea about what business you are in and where you want to be going with that business, only then can you begin to set a strategy for achieving those ends.

1 www.teal.org.uk

2 www.worldvision.org.uk

3 Faith communities should note that Core Values are not the same as a doctrinal statement. These are very different and equally important declarations, but they deal with separate issues.

4 www.givingthebest.co.uk

5 Courtney (2002).

6 Lewis Caroll (1865) *Alice in Wonderland.*

10   Choosing what not to do first

'The essence of strategy is choosing what not to do.'
Michael Porter

Before you started reading this book, you were probably running around spinning all the plates, dropping a few here and there, and starting each day with the agonising question of *'What in the world am I going to do first?'* By encouraging you to plan strategically, you will know the answer to that question because you have a plan, and that plan gives you priorities. I hope you are breathing a sigh of relief in anticipation of actually achieving that glorious state!

In the previous chapters, we began the process of examining the five key statements that make up the strategic purpose. We have looked at *Purpose*, *Values* and *Vision*. We come now to the final two; the *Strategic Plan* and *Objectives*. (Yes, I know; in Chapter 8, Figure 3 I showed six elements, not five – but as we will see shortly, the *Fundraising Plan* is really part of the overall *Strategic Plan*.)

Reality check

The dilemma which faces those who are responsible for the management of small charities has been expressed as a combination of the following:

* Limited resources – not enough funds, not enough donors
* Limited staff – it's just you and your wife
* Limited skills – you don't know what to do about it.

These limitations are sometimes compounded by the fact that one person is doing everything and that there are only 24 hours in each day. Unless the problem is approached *strategically* (remember, that means looking at the *bigger picture*), you will probably run out of energy and ideas all at the same time.

Planning strategically

I have already made the point that many small charities do not have a workable *Strategic Plan*; they are simply responding to whichever opportunity raises its head at the moment, or grabbing the most attractive-looking project that looms over the horizon. These projects or opportunities may not be bad in themselves – they may well be in line with the overall *Purpose* – but strategy is about focusing your energies to concentrate on the most important issues, the ones that will use your resources to the maximum effect so that you achieve your charitable objectives in the most efficient manner. In short, you have to sort out your priorities. And that is strategic in itself.

If having a *Vision* is like choosing your destination, then setting a *Strategic Plan* is planning the route on a map. There may be more than one option, but you need to choose the one that looks best when all factors are taken into consideration. It may be that in the course of the journey, surprises crop up (such as traffic jams ahead, or accidents) that necessitate modifying the route. But the destination is still going to be the same. It is the same with a good *Strategic Plan*. It needs to stay flexible; able to be modified if circumstances dictate. But one thing is certain – it will always be heading towards achieving the *Vision* and *Purpose*.

I want to keep this section really simple, and approach the issue of developing a strategy at the most basic level. You probably do not have the time right now to study this at MBA level. If you do, there are numerous management guides on how to do this, but you can easily make the whole thing far too complicated. It's not rocket science. It's about understanding where you want to go, and writing down how you want to get there.

So who's the navigator?

Who is going to write your strategic plan? The more members of your team who are involved in the process, the better the chance you have of everyone buying into the concept. The CEO who creates a plan in isolation without consulting the rest of the team is going to face an uphill struggle in ensuring that everyone owns the final plan. On the other hand, you don't want an unwieldy committee, the sort that sets out to design a horse and invents a camel. Certainly the CEO and any senior management team should be involved in the process, but consideration should be given to asking each member of staff for their contributions too. Maybe you will want to ask them at the outset 'Where would you like to see the organisation in three years time?' or 'What would make the most significant difference to the way we achieve our charitable objects?' Every department should be represented at an early stage so that no one feels left out or disenfranchised. Staff representation is vital for buy-in and implementation.

Key result areas

You should start by identifying about 5 *Key Result Areas* (KRAs) that you want to achieve. KRAs are simply 'areas where you need to see key results in your work'. A KRA might be operational, such as better training for the staff that run your drop-in centre, or it might be focused on resourcing, such as developing a donor database. In fact, they could well be a combination of any of the four Critical Success Factors of the Triangle; service delivery, fundraising, governance, and executive.

Under each of the KRAs, list the following:

- **Outcomes** – what exactly are we trying to achieve? What will be the tangible benefits in terms of our Purpose and Charitable Objects?

- **Responsibility** – who is going to take the lead on this? Are we spreading the load fairly between us?

- **Resources** – what is the budget for this project? Do we need to recruit more staff to achieve success? Do we need some extra help from outside?

- **Timings** – realistically, when will this be accomplished?

- **Performance Indicators** – how will we measure what we are doing, or if we are failing to hit the mark?

You can easily tabulate this list, or you might find it easier to write short paragraphs under the headings given. Either way, you should aim to produce a concise document that will be easily read and understood by all members of the team.

All I want for Christmas

At this stage it will become obvious that you can't simply create a 'Santa's Wish List' for everything you want to achieve operationally during the first 12 months. The resourcing implications dictate that you can only develop your service delivery function if you have the people in place to develop the fundraising at the same pace. This is the primary rule of the Triangle of Sustainability.

So, a typical list of KRAs for a small emerging charity might be:

1. To appoint a full-time chief executive within 12 months.
2. To create a database with 1,000 supporters within 2 years.
3. To re-launch the website with an online donation facility.
4. To open 2 new TB clinics within 3 years.
5. To train 5 new case workers per year.

You will notice that only items 4 and 5 deal with service delivery function. Items 1-3 are all about the executive and fundraising, but without which the service delivery will not function. These issues need to be dealt with piecemeal, and like the proverbial 'How do you eat an elephant?' the answer is 'One bite at a time'.

Clarifying objectives

Having the basics of a strategic plan is not going to produce the goods all on its own; you have to make sure that it is put into practice. This is where you need the last of the five elements of the strategic process: the *Objectives* (or *Goals*). You now need to set down what needs to be done, by when and by whom. You can do this as a time-line chart or critical path analysis chart. This will help you to make sure that you plan things in the right order.

This is a very exciting stage for you; you are getting somewhere at last! It does not have to be perfect or 100% complete to start using your strategic plan. A rough draft is better than no plan at all. But as long as things are moving forward because you are planning for it to happen, instead of simply reacting to crisis and events around you, there is a very good chance of achieving stability. The Triangle isn't going to collapse at one side after all.

Structure and strategy are critical to success

A sound *structure* is as vital as the *strategy*. But strategic thinking is necessary in order to identify the structure. When this involves increasing staff levels, the strategy can require some bold moves on behalf of the trustees. In the next chapter we shall be looking more at the structure of the organisation.

If you are the founder and your skills are particularly focused on service delivery activities, you might be tempted to ignore the needs for strategic planning because the vital work 'on the field' is just too attractive. It is too easy to plod on doing the things that might have worked in the past, or appear to be working well for other organisations, until these strategies come unstuck.

In Chapter 2, the four main functions of the Triangle of Sustainability were described as *Critical Success Factors*. Each of these four functions, *Service Delivery, Fundraising, Governance* and the *Executive* are critical to the success of your organisation. The development of each of these will not happen unless there is a proactive strategy for ensuring that they are developed. The temptation for the founder is usually to run away with ideas on *Service Delivery*. It is easy to make plans for new clinics and orphanages. It is not so exciting to write induction manuals for newly appointed Board members or to co-ordinate a direct mail campaign.

It's always a balancing act

What you need to be thinking about daily is that by giving all these issues the priority that they deserve, the ultimate goal of helping some very needy people or worthy cause is going to be greatly enhanced. You have to balance your time and effort in accordance with the Triangle. It's equal measures all round from now on. A charity without a strategic plan is like an aeroplane without wings; it isn't going anywhere.

Digging deep

One of my hobbies is my vegetable garden. Aside from the therapeutic value of gardening, the ultimate aim is to enjoy eating home-grown food. However, before I can achieve that goal there is a lot of digging and weeding to be done. I always remind myself that it will be worth the effort when it comes to harvest time, and it is the same with much of the hard work for planning and implementing strategic groundwork in the voluntary sector. Keep reminding yourself of why you are doing it. The photo of the children in the orphanage on your desk, the framed Purpose Statement on the office wall will keep you focused.

The fundraising plan

Part of the strategic process is to create a fundraising plan. If you are in leadership in a voluntary organisation which is motivated by the acute needs of your beneficiaries, you are probably not at a loss to think of ideas to address those needs. Your biggest struggle will no doubt be how to *resource* those ideas. Where will you find the people to do the work, and ultimately, where will the funds come from to sustain it?

There are three questions you need to ask yourself before you start fundraising:

1 **What do you do?** – What is your Purpose? What is your Vision? We have already addressed these questions in Chapters 8-9.

2 **How much does it cost you to do it?** – What are your fixed costs, variable costs, core costs, capital costs, etc? This will be apparent as you complete your strategic plan.

3 **Who is going to pay for it?** – This is the area we are now going to look at, but it presupposes you have in fact answered questions 1 and 2, without which you will be grasping at straws.

The Case for Support

The bedrock of all fundraising strategies is the *Case for Support*. This is an internal management tool that tries to answer the question 'Why should I want to support your cause?' It will present the necessary background facts about the organisation and the campaign in a single brief document of no more than two sides of A4. This Case for Support will include:

- Who you are and what is your purpose?
- What are the specific objectives of your campaign?
- Why is your campaign important and urgent?
- What are the implications if you do not embark on this course of action?
- How much are you trying to raise?
- Over what period of time are you planning to fundraise?
- Who else is contributing?

Sam Clarke, a former Director of Fundraising at Oxfam, has expressed it this way:

'What exactly is the need? What are the consequences or implications of this need? And what will happen if nothing is done about it? ... If the need is not important and your role is not clear, developing a good 'case' becomes very difficult.' [1]

Once you have an agreed Case for Support, all appeals, whether to individual donors or applications to grant-making trusts, will be 'singing from the same song sheet'. You will be consistent in expressing both the needs and the solutions to each need.

The Income Mix

The next stage is to identify potential sources of income – we call this the *Income Mix* – and it may well differ from cause to cause. The income mix may be made up of the following:

- Individual donors
- Grant-making trusts
- Government agencies
- The corporate sector
- Churches or other organisations
- Trading activities

The secret now is to identify which of the above will be appropriate for your charity and create a strategy for reaching your budgeted targets through an income mix of these groups.

Experience has shown that the majority of your income will come from 'individuals', typically around 80% is the norm. Some charities have made the mistake of relying on Government contracts, or they believe in a fairy godmother called 'Grandmother Grant Maker' who will just wave her magic wand whenever the charity needs more funds. Grants are vitally important, but they are increasingly hard to come by, require much hard work and research to acquire, and even when successful, produce huge unpredictable peaks and troughs in your cash flow.

The way around this is to steadily build up a trickle of regular income from individual donors, who might only be able to give very small amounts compared to the income you might get from a grant. A steady flow of smaller but regular gifts from individual donors can produce a reliable and predictable cash flow that will enable you to plan your operational budget from year to year. You may be a provider of social welfare or an arts group that does not appear to have many individual 'supporters' or 'members'. However, income from 'individuals' also includes funds received from legacies, fundraising events that interface with the general public, direct mail campaigns, radio and TV appeals, and many more activities that can produce income from the wider public, not just your core supporters.

We are getting towards the stage where you will be ready to incorporate a fundraising plan into your overall strategic plan. Figure 4 sets out graphically how this will be accomplished. I have already explained how the strategic process leads from a clear sense of Purpose, Values and Vision and produces a strategic plan that leads to Objectives (or Goals). The Fundraising Plan is part of the Strategic Plan and sets out how the strategy is going to be resourced. Having completed a Case for Support, sources of funding are identified from the Income Mix and targets are set for how much is realistically expected to be found from each source. Like all good business plans, monitoring and review will be imperative as the plan progresses.

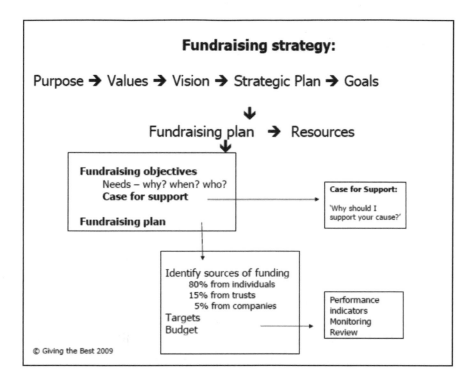

Figure 4

I said at the outset that this is like following a map to your destination. If I am driving up the A1 to see my family in Yorkshire, and I run into a traffic jam or accident on route, a quick look at my map tells me I can also get there via the M1, so I make the necessary diversion – but we are still going to Yorkshire, nowhere else. Do not be afraid to make changes as you learn from experience what is working well for your situation and what is not.

We now have a plan to get to our destination, but we need to choose who else is coming with us on the journey. Recruiting the right team is going to be vital.

---

1 Clarke and Norton (1997), p.276.

 **Team dynamics**

'Surround yourself with the best people you can find, delegate authority … and don't interfere.'
Ronald Reagan

You will have gathered that I am on a personal campaign to help founders move away from being a one-person charity, where they are doing everything themselves and probably only treading water. You should now be thinking about drawing in non-trustees to do the administration and other tasks. Perhaps there will be volunteers in this role to begin with, but in time you will probably want to employ someone, and the Triangle will start to grow. You've dug the ground well, you have watered your seeds – expect to see something coming up green soon!

Back in late spring this year, I helped my four-year-old grandson plant some seeds in his vegetable plot. He had to learn that they were not going to become beetroot and broccoli overnight. It was going to take some patience and a lot of personal care. I was eager, come the summer, to go back and see how well he had learned both of those skills.

Building your team
Likewise, you will not be able to achieve team-building overnight, and this is where Strategic Planning is so important. It should be your long-term goal to progress from being a one-person show doing everything yourself, to having people with the correct skills and experience filling key roles in management and administration.

The international NGO of which I was once Chair had no full-time UK staff when I joined the Board. One of the trustees was filling the role of part-time Director, with some part-time secretarial help. We realised that the organisation would never move beyond just 'ticking over' with that kind of structure, so we took the bold step of advertising for a full-time Director. The key issue was that we couldn't really afford to pay a salary, but instead of letting this become the stumbling block, the trustees decided that we would personally take on the commitment to raise 6 months' worth of salary from our various personal contacts, in the belief that once in place, the new role would generate enough income to self-sustain.

This is exactly what happened. We appointed a very gifted person in the role and he has been able to develop a secure funding base which not only covers his salary but has allowed the appointment of three other UK staff members since. We were also able to increase the charitable expenditure on service delivery. It was very hard work, but it would never have happened unless we as trustees had not taken the bold step to move forward.

Classic human resource management teaching says that staffing requirements must be subordinate to strategy. You set your strategy and then recruit the staff to implement it. But in practice, what you've got is what you've got. Or more precisely, *who* you've got. You may find yourself being forced into building a plan around the team you have inherited, with their particular strengths and weaknesses. It is not ideal. But which of us ever lives in an ideal world?

Step one, as we saw in the last two chapters, should be to identify the organisation's goals and the strategy for reaching them. Step two is to prepare a *'human capital plan'* that indicates what kinds of people with what kinds of talents will be able to carry out the strategy. You can apply this process to your embryonic strategic plan for your charity.

Deciding where help is needed

Make a list of everything you do for just one week. At the end of that week, ask yourself which of those tasks should have been done by someone else. You will quickly draw up the profile of the person that you need to recruit. You might want to start with some volunteer help with the administration — someone who is great with the computer, who can produce letters, update the mailing lists, check the bank statements, and so on.

Keep going back to the Triangle of Sustainability. Only expand in administrative areas in proportion to the work being done with your beneficiaries. But never let the front-line work overtake the need for adequate back-room support.

Team priorities

When thinking through your 'Human Capital Plan', these are the 3 areas you should be thinking about investing in as a priority:

1. **Administration and bookkeeping** – someone who is happy to spend time working with figures and pouring over spreadsheets. This will allow you to keep your eyes fixed on wider issues of running the charity.

2. **Database administration** – although this requires someone with IT skills, they should also be relational, because they will spend much of their time communicating with donors. It is not a good idea to combine the two roles of bookkeeping and database management for that reason.

3. **A fundraiser** – we will need to look at this area in more detail below.

Hopefully by now you should be a little clearer on what your own role is. You might have been able to shake off the mantle of Chair of Trustees and settle for Chief Executive. This role might turn out to be Director of Fundraising under another name. I see so many adverts for charity Directors or Chief Executives that are really only fundraising roles. A recent survey conducted at the Institute of Fundraising Annual Convention in 2010 asked charity Chief Executives what their top three challenges were. *'Income Generation'* came out way on top of the list, and yet most the job holders were from an operational background, and did not have fundraising experience.[1]

Are you really cut out for fundraising? Do you have any real experience in this area? Eventually, you should be appointing a dedicated fundraiser as a member of your team if you are serious about the charity growing. Just as you may have realised that Governance is not your strong point, maybe the time has come – or will be just around the corner – for you to stop doing the fundraising too. Not that fundraising is a particularly difficult task – anyone can do it once they have learnt the 'rules of the game'. But not everyone has the motivation to do it. And if this is not you, then you need to find someone else for that role.

Developing and managing your fundraiser

Fundraisers are usually specialists in specific areas, such as direct mail, event management, legacy campaigns, grants and foundations or corporate affairs. You will probably only be able to afford to add one person to the team at once. If you can find someone with experience in all of the above areas you will be very fortunate – but they will probably be senior enough to want a salary way beyond what you had in mind. Actually, you would probably prefer not to be paying them anything at this stage – but it's time to move into the real world!

An alternative approach, which I have used successfully on several occasions, is to recruit someone who has a couple of years' experience in one of these specialist areas with a large charity. They will be young enough to want to develop their skills, and enthusiastic enough to want to get involved with an emerging enterprise like yours. Personality is perhaps just as important as experience. You will want a self-starter, but one who is easy to manage. A marketing degree would be excellent – marketing and fundraising go very well together and it is easy to transfer skills from one to the other. Several of my clients have recruited someone like this and I have taken a year or so to mentor them as they grow into quite proficient fundraising managers. The total outlay of their salary plus my consultancy fee for a day each month is much less than having to pay the salary of an experienced senior fundraiser.

Fundraisers work with money; so do accountants. But fundraisers should never work *for* accountants. Accountants, by necessity, are detailed, methodical people who stick to the rules, for very legitimate reasons. Fundraisers are continually pushing the boundaries and are much more likely to be creative, people-orientated types. If your fundraiser is being line-managed by your accountant, you take the risk of destroying the fundraiser's creativity, which is their core strength. Your accountant could well be taking time off through stress, too!

I know you think that you can't afford to employ anybody just yet, but it's a chicken and egg scenario. It may be that you can't afford NOT to employ someone. It is generally agreed that any fundraising appointment should eventually be generating at least five times its cost to the organisation. Many are producing much more than that, especially people working on legacy campaigns or major donor strategies.

So back to the Triangle – hold off on spending any more on Service Delivery for say six months, while you invest on strengthening this vital corner of the structure. If all goes well, and you get the right person on board, in twelve months' time you should be exceeding your current income to a level where you have recovered any losses made by taking on an extra member of staff. If you would prefer to think in sporting terms, imagine a Formula One Grand Prix. Lewis Hamilton is out in front by 3 seconds, but he really needs to change his tyres. The temptation to carry on with the wrong tyres is strong, but eventually the new treads will enable him to quickly recover the lost seconds that he spent in the pits putting it right.

You want to be on the winner's podium? Pull over now!

Using volunteers

I have already suggested using volunteer help to cover some of the vital tasks that might need undertaking. Having volunteers to help with the volume of work needed to move the charity forward towards self-sufficiency is both cost-effective and appropriate in terms of human resources. But there are real risks involved with using volunteers, and this next section will include advice on identifying those risks and present ideas in order to mitigate any risk to the charity.

Volunteers may not be salaried but that does not mean they come as 'freebies'. They need managing and resourcing; both have real costs. Volunteers can enable the charity to grow at a much faster rate because they will hopefully engage with their own circle of friends and contacts, thus multiplying the potential interest. In time, some of these volunteers might want to move into a more permanent relationship with you. It is quite usual in the life-cycle of charities for the paid staff to be recruited from among those who worked as volunteers in the first instance. Some essential advice on managing volunteers is available from the National Council for Voluntary Organisations (NCVO) website. NCVO warns against creating 'contracts', as this can blur the distinction between paid staff and volunteers.

'When the distinction between volunteer and employee becomes blurred, voluntary organisations can find themselves with legal problems. In a number of recent claims, voluntary workers won the right to be considered as employees and brought a claim against their 'employers' for both discrimination and unfair dismissal.' [2]

However, it's important to give the volunteer clear guidelines on what he or she can do, particularly when it comes to ensuring that they avoid breaking the laws on fundraising, or working with children and other vulnerable people.

Claiming expenses

It is also essential that every volunteer abides by a strict financial policy. They should understand that expenses will be reimbursed for agreed out-of-pocket items at rates laid down, on production of receipts. Expense claim forms can be produced. Most charities find that volunteers are hesitant about claiming expenses, particularly if they are for small amounts. They like to think that this is part of their contribution to the cause. It feels penny-pinching to claim for petty expenses when the charity is struggling to raise funds. However, charity accounting practice, SORP, requires that all expenses are budgeted and shown in the accounts even if the volunteer decides to waive their right to claim them.[3] The expense claim form can list the amounts claimed (such as telephone calls, private mileage) and then the volunteer can sign a declaration waiving this claim. The total amount then becomes a donation to the charity and should be shown in the accounts as both an income and an expense, even though no cash has actually changed hands. The reason this is important is that the full cost of fundraising needs to be accounted for, including expenses incurred by volunteers and staff.

Volunteers also need to understand that they can not simply deduct their expenses from any income received from a fundraising event. All income generated at events must be paid gross into the charity's bank account, and expenses claimed separately.

Managing volunteers is different

Consideration needs to be given to who will oversee the team of volunteers. Most charities find this area of their work to be a challenge. Volunteers, by nature, can be hard to manage. They do not always want to conform to policies or procedures and like to keep their non-employee status very clear. Various training courses are available from the Directory of Social Change and other training providers on how to manage a successful volunteer team. References should be obtained for all volunteers prior to their commencing work, and a probationary period, of say three months, should be the norm before confirming any appointment. Releasing unsatisfactory volunteers is sometimes more difficult than firing an employee. One charity found that a volunteer, who was told their services were no longer required, continued to speak at meetings 'on behalf' of the charity because they enjoyed doing so!

Pruning the team

Up to now, I have been talking in terms of adding staff to your team. I am talking growth. But just as my fruit bushes only continue to bear good fruit if I cut out the dead wood, it may well be that your organisation already needs some pruning work. You may discover as you start to implement your strategy that you have staff you don't need, either because they are just not up to the task or they are surplus to requirements. The voluntary sector has always been a little negligent by comparison to the business sector when it comes to laying-off staff. Perhaps it is because we are so focussed on meeting human need that we feel that making staff redundant is counter-culture. Nevertheless, in terms of meeting the needs of your beneficiaries, reducing core costs by eliminating unnecessary posts can mean more funds available for meeting your charitable objects.

Typically, established charities find that 50-60% of their expenditure budget is taken up by salaries. Reducing those fixed costs by even one post can often make a huge difference to the sustainability of the organisation. You will need to consult a legal adviser or human resources expert before considering any redundancies because this is another area where it can become a minefield if you get it wrong.

Team role dynamics

The Triangle, if properly implemented, will bring in team members with different skills sets. These people will probably each have different personalities and social profiles. In any team event there are likely to be specialists. Football, rugby, hockey – whatever your sport. No football team can succeed with eleven Wayne Rooneys. He's a striker, a classic centre forward, by the way, in case you are not into football. Defenders are needed too, as is an experienced goalkeeper – it's the same in a successful charity. One of your goals – no pun intended – should be to bring in people who complement each other's skills.

Identifying team roles

Dr R Meredith Belbin, Visiting Professor at Henley Management College, has identified nine clusters of behaviour, termed Team Roles. Each Team Role has its own strengths and weaknesses, and each makes its own contribution to the overall success of the team. The advantage of using the Belbin material is that it allows people to work to their strengths and weaknesses. You don't need to go on expensive management courses to discover where your strengths and weakness lie. Belbin has a number of self-perception inventories and team games available on his website which can be achieved easily and inexpensively downloaded.[4]

The Team Roles he has identified are listed on page 88 (Figure 5).

Belbin is quick to stress that these roles are not necessary 'personality types'. Although there are nine separate roles, some of them are compatible and can be assumed by the same person. Some are very much non-compatible. You will usually need at least four people in your team if you want to cover all the Team Roles.

Creator or completer?

I find myself to be very comfortable in the *Plant* and *Specialist* roles, but certainly not in the *Completer Finisher* role. I am full of new creative ideas,

1	Plant	A creative, imaginative, unorthodox team member who solves difficult problems. Although they sometimes situate themselves far from the other team members, they always come back to present their 'brilliant' idea.
2	Resource Investigator	The networker for the group. Whatever the team needs, he/she is likely to have someone in their address book that can either provide it or knows someone else who can provide it.
3	Chairman/ Co-ordinator	Ensures that all members of the team are able to contribute to discussions and decisions of the team. Their concern is for fairness and equity among team members.
4	Shaper	A dynamic team member who loves a challenge and thrives on pressure.
5	Monitor-Evaluator	A sober, strategic and discerning member who tries to see all options and judges accurately. This member contributes a measured and dispassionate analysis and, through objectivity, stops the team committing itself to a misguided task.
6	Team Worker	Ensures that interpersonal relationships within the team are maintained. Sensitive to atmospheres and may be the first to approach another team member who feels slighted, excluded or otherwise attacked, but has not expressed their discomfort.
7	Implementer	The practical thinker who can create systems and processes that will produce what the team wants. Taking a problem and working out how it can be practically addressed is their strength.
8	Completer Finisher	The detail person within the team. They have a great eye for spotting flaws and gaps and for knowing exactly where the team is in relation to its schedule.
9	Specialist	Brings 'specialist' knowledge to the team.

Figure 5
Reproduced by kind permission of Belbin Associates, UK

and have lots of energy to initiate them and inspire others to join in, but I prefer to hand over the task to others once the job becomes routine. My experiences in the community group I started illustrate this. Once the initial set-up work was done, I was very keen to hand over the running of the group to another leader who was more of a *Completer Finisher*.

Having spent some time as Chairman of an international charity, I have to confess that I found it hard work ensuring that all other members of the Board were able to contribute equally to the discussions and decisions made. I like to think I did a pretty good job of being the Chair, but it wasn't my natural strong point. There were many times when I had to hold back on my own tendency to want to bring my own views to the table, in order to facilitate others to do so. Being the Chair is not an excuse for exerting control.

What really motivates you?

Bryn Hughes, in *Leadership Tool Kit*, uses the theories of American sociologist David McClelland to explain what he calls *Primary Social Motives*.[5] According to McClelland, we are all motivated by a combination of three primary motives; the need for *Achievement*, the need for *Affiliation* (or relationships) and the need for *Power* (or influence). Again, like the Belbin models, these are not positive or negative traits, they just describe the way we all prefer to work. The Achiever will be happiest in working down a list of tasks to accomplish. The Affiliate will work best in a team with others around them. The Power/Influence person enjoys getting results by influencing others. All these people can be successful in your team. You need to ensure that whatever tasks you assign to your team members they are matched to their Primary Social Motives. I love working down check lists and completing reports. I am an Achiever. When I attend networking sessions with groups of people I don't know, I find myself hanging back because I am not that motivated by Affiliation; I can do it for a while but I am working outside my comfort zone. 'Power' people can be hard to manage, especially if you, as their line manager, are not so motivated by Power. The secret is to give them opportunities to teach and mentor others, and keep telling them how their work is making an impact.

Role play

I once had to switch the roles of two girls working in the office. One was an Achiever and she hated her job on reception. The phone kept interrupting her typing tasks! Meanwhile, her friend, who was high on Affiliation and who had the task of updating the technical manuals, was going crazy standing by the photocopier all day because she didn't talk to anyone. We simply switched their roles and they were both not only much happier, but their output improved dramatically.

The most important thing to remember as you build your team according to the Triangle of Sustainability is that the team is subservient to the needs of the ultimate beneficiaries. You only exist in order to meet their requirements. The organisation itself will cease to exist when all their needs are met. Some organisations grow not only in size but also in their perception of their own importance, and in doing so they forget that in the voluntary sector, we are all servants of a wider cause. As the Triangle grows in equilibrium, keeping governance, management and resourcing in balance with service delivery, a degree of humility and self-sacrifice will also be necessary to balance the successes and a natural sense of pride that comes with it.

---

1 Third Sector 20 July 2010, p.31.
2 www.ncvo-vol.org.uk
3 Statement of Recommended Practice.
4 www.belbin.com
5 Hughes (1998), pp.66-77.

12 The future looks bright

'The work goes on, the cause endures, the hope still lives and the dreams shall never die.'
Edward Kennedy

If you have made it this far you have hopefully grasped the concepts of planning strategically. You have understood the principle of keeping the Triangle sustainable by expanding each area of your work interdependently. You will have also decided which aspects of fundraising are appropriate for your cause and what you want to do first. Since this book is intended as an ongoing source of reference, maybe you have already put some of that into practice and you are now reading this later on in a new light. If this is the case, it is probably time to be looking at some of the other important issues which will keep your charity moving forward and prevent it from grinding to a halt at the first plateau.

Getting the best from your website

When I take on a new client, I want to learn everything I can about them. I will usually check to see if they have a website, as this not only gives me some factual background about the work, but it also tells me an enormous amount by the way it is presented. Because small charities are usually cash strapped, many have fallen into the trap of either designing their website in-house by using one of the many home-made templates available, or they have allowed a friend-of-a-friend (or worse, a relative of a trustee!) to design one for them. These well-meaning friends are more often quite competent in the technical bells and whistles of making sure the web pages function when you click the appropriate button, but if they don't know what they are doing with marketing and branding principles, they may have done you a disservice.

Having your own website needn't be an expensive option for the small charity. You can easily have a simple website designed professionally for around £1,000. Larger agencies are going to charge more, but there are plenty of self-employed designers working from home who can give you a competitive quote. Always look at their portfolio of work already done and see if you like their style.

Creating a 'Brand Image'

Find a graphic designer who will create a strong brand image for you that can be used on all your publicity, letterheads, business cards etc. The logo needs to be easily recognised and be sensitive to your cause. Get them to produce several options, and if you don't like any of them, send them back literally to the drawing board.

Think about what you want on your website from the perspective of the users. I am sorry, but if I want to find out quickly about your work because I am thinking of making a donation to you, or I am considering coming to an event you are organising, the last thing I want see on your home page is a long biography of yourself, the founder, or history of the organisation. I want to know quickly what you do, where you do it, and how I can get involved. Keep words to a minimum.

Netting your catch

I use the internet for almost everything these days. I do all my Christmas shopping online, I bank online, I communicate with my family through social networks, and I plan and book my holidays online. I know what I want from a website, and so do you. If the page doesn't load quickly, or it doesn't grab my attention in what I am looking for in the first few seconds, I will go somewhere else where it does. So make sure your message is clear and easy to read on the very first page that pops up. Be careful in the use of colour. Lots of white space always works best. Keep it simple, and avoid 'flash' technology at all costs. It is estimated that around 25-30% of internet users are now accessing the web via mobile phones. Check to see that your web design works on an i-Phone or Blackberry. Remember also to make your website accessible for those who have difficulties with eyesight.[1]

Once you have your site designed professionally, you can then select a technical agency to host it for you. Again this need not be expensive – I am paying around £90 a year for a hosting service which includes the provision of email accounts.[2]

Having a professional appearance to your website will immediately tell potential donors and service users alike that you are a serious player and not just the local tiddlywinks club (nothing wrong with a tiddlywinks club, really).

Do remember that UK websites are now considered to be adverts and therefore have to observe the British Codes of Advertising, Sales Promotion and Direct Marketing, which say that *'adverts must be legal, decent, honest and truthful'*.[3] It may be a criminal offence if your website describes the services you are providing (or want to provide) in a misleading or exaggerated way in order to solicit donations. To describe your organisation as having *'a team of dedicated clinical specialists throughout Africa'* when in fact, you only have two nurses working in Johannesburg and a doctor who might be joining them sometime next year, is wishful thinking, and could get you into trouble.

Online donations

It will be important to have *online donation* facilities built into your website. It is not worth paying for the development of a secure bespoke system since there are several excellent providers available now. The fees charged for this service are quite reasonable and since they provide a secure service with Gift Aid collected at source, it is usually more cost-effective than trying to do it yourself in-house. Do compare their prices though. Is there a set-up cost? Is there an ongoing subscription? What do they charge for a credit card versus a debit card use? Can you personalise your webpage to include your own logo and branding? How quickly will they pass your donations on to you?

It is well worth looking at other people's sites to see how they look and how they work. It is even worth sending a few pounds to one or two other charities to see how easily their online donation facilities function and how quickly their gift acknowledgment process works. One particular provider functions like a credit card company and only sends statements out to the recipient charities once a month. The donor could easily be kept waiting for

6 weeks for a 'thank you' letter. The two leading providers in this field will inform the charity immediately for every gift received. I once sponsored a friend in a sporting event to encourage him and received the automated email reply within seconds of making my donation. Within a few minutes, I had also received a personal 'thank you' from my friend which told me they had informed him too. That is good service and well worth paying for. You can also get online donation facilities free, which might be tempting, but you get what you pay for and you may be disappointed with the service provided.

Personal development

By now you are probably also realising the value of learning as much as you can from others around you 'in the trade'. I try to attend training or networking sessions at least once a month in order to keep sharp and up to date on the constant changes that are happening in the voluntary sector. For me, the best value is through membership of the *Institute of Fundraising*. Not only does it provide excellent training courses which lead to recognised qualifications in fundraising, but members get substantial discounts on events and services. There are a number of Special Interest Groups that focus specifically on key areas of fundraising. The Codes of Best Practice produced by the Institute are considered to be the recognised industry standard and will greatly enhance the credibility of your organisation. By attending regular functions of the Institute you will quickly get to know who is who in the sector as well as becoming known yourself. This is very valuable when you want to cross-check new ideas with another member.

If you are the founder and your skills are focused on the service delivery, you may want to invest in some training and get qualifications in fundraising or in managing a voluntary organisation. Again there are several options for either one or two-day courses run by the Directory of Social Change, right up to MBA and PhD level studies at places such as the Cass Business School at the University of London or the London South Bank University. Not many of us who call ourselves 'professional' fundraisers planned our careers to end up this way. We morphed into the trade via the operational side of charity work. But having done so, we have found it to be extremely rewarding, and we want our work to be under-girded by excellence.

Investment in training is not a piece of self-indulgence; it is an essential part of making sure you bring added value to the cause.

Legacy campaigns

One valuable course which you might want to consider attending is in planning and managing a *legacy campaign*. I have deliberately left this section until the last chapter, because a legacy campaign is probably not going to be an immediate priority for an emerging new charity. However, it should be a vital piece of your long-term strategy. If you need an urgent injection of short-term cash, the answer could be a direct mail appeal letter. Grants from trusts will produce medium-term results, but legacies are your long term security. Legacy income is completely unpredictable, and as a general rule should not be expected to produce fruit within the first 3-4 years from the launch of the campaign. However, the sums involved can be significant over the long term. Perhaps more importantly, legacy income is usually unrestricted and can be used for core funding.

Any legacy campaign must be properly managed in order to succeed. The major cancer charities and hospices in the UK receive millions of pounds annually via legacies. This is not just because those who die of cancer tend to leave their money to cancer research. These agencies have dedicated teams to promote legacy giving. Many charities produce a tasteful booklet or brochure giving their supporters information about the legal aspects of writing a Will. All this is good, but what many of them forget to do is to actually ask their donors if they will include the charity in their Will. It is not something to be embarrassed about. There is clear evidence to show that legacies are most often left to the charities that have asked their supporters to consider this as an option.

If you don't ask...

Roger was the CEO of a residential home for adults with learning disabilities and I was helping him to develop his fundraising strategy. One of their residents was a middle-aged man who had been with them for over 14 years when he was sadly diagnosed with cancer and died very quickly. For the last two weeks of his life he was in the care of a local hospice. Roger was devastated to discover that the family had left a memorial bequest to the hospice that had cared for this man for just two weeks and ignored those who had provided 14 years of love and support. I told my client the bare facts: 'It wasn't because the family thought you hadn't cared for their son – it was simply because the hospice asked for the legacy and you didn't!'

Risk management

If you have already put in place some of these ideas, then hopefully your Triangle is becoming more sustainable and not likely to topple. There will always be crisis days of course. Things do not always go according to plan, and when the unexpected happens, it helps if you have already thought through some of the issues ahead of time. If your trustees have put in place a robust risk assessment, you will already have looked at what possibly might go wrong and what steps you have taken to mitigate the risks to the charity if they were to occur.

The methodology I like to employ when it comes to *Risk Management* is to sit down with the whole staff and draw up a list of everything you can imagine that might possibly go wrong, including things like a fire or flood in the office, theft of computers, fraudulent use of data, key people taking long-term sick leave, and so on. You will be surprised at how creative the staff can be when dreaming up disasters! Then you tabulate against each possibility a score out of 5 of the chances of that happening, with 1 being a low risk and 5 a very high possibility. In the next column, give another score out of 5 of the effect within the organisation if it were to happen, with 1 being very little adverse effect and 5 being a disaster. Multiply the two scores together to give a total risk score. This will help you identify the greatest areas of risk – obviously anything approaching a score of 25 needs urgent attention! In the final column you should list the steps you are taking to mitigate those risks to the organisation, such as *'back-up files made weekly and stored off-site.'*

There are some crises that can be turned around into a success story for you. Do not allow the negative aspects of a disaster to create bad PR among your supporters. For instance, one of your volunteers is tragically killed in an accident in a developing country. Do not wait for their relatives to feed the media with untruths about inadequate training and supervision, blaming your organisation for neglect. Get in first with a press release saying what a great loss this is going to be for the organisation and how this dedicated volunteer was making a world of difference to the beneficiaries.

If you are facing a cash flow crisis, the last thing you should do is write to your supporters telling them that unless they bail you out now, the work will stop. It probably isn't true anyway, but even if it were, donors do not like to be part of failures; we all prefer to be part of a success story. Find a way of telling your story from a positive angle so that your donors want to do more of a good thing.

Reserves policy

Surviving a cash flow crisis is exactly why you should have a *reserves policy* that allows you to survive a few weeks or months of unexpected decline. A few years ago, one large UK relief agency was the target of a TV slur, which was eventually refuted (and cost the TV company dearly in an out-of-court settlement). However, in the meantime, hundreds of loyal donors had cancelled their standing orders, having believed the untruths that were being fed to them by the media. Fortunately, the charity concerned managed the crisis through having free-reserves of cash. They were able to ride out those difficult weeks when income dipped below that which was needed to pay salaries and keep projects ticking over. A surprising number of charities, when faced with cash shortfall during the recession that hit in 2008/9, were reluctant to dip into their reserves to see them through. Reserves, they reasoned, were 'there for emergencies'. To my mind, a cash flow crisis caused by the worst global downturn in living memory is probably as bad an emergency as you will ever need!

The Triangle still rules. OK?

A crisis needn't be the cause of the Triangle toppling though. Having the right people in governance and management who are prepared to take tough decisions, talking to supporters and beneficiaries alike, delaying unnecessary spending when cash flow is tight; all these things will lead to sustainability. Your strategic plan, we have said, is like a road map. You are on a journey and when the unexpected happens en route, you need to consult the map to see if there is an alternate route that can get you to the same destination. Don't be afraid to make changes to your plan if it is not working. Put things on hold, go back to things that have worked well for you in the past. But do keep your eyes on the ultimate goal and don't allow panic to introduce any element of strategic drift.

How's it going?

Whether you go through bad times or not, periodically you will want to get away with your senior team, maybe invite some trustees along too, and ask yourselves: 'How are we doing?' Here are some starters that you might want to work through as you evaluate your effectiveness:

- Are we meeting our stated Charitable Objects?
- Are we being faithful to our Purpose Statement?
- Are our Values understood and implemented by the whole team?
- Where are we along the journey of achieving our Vision?
- Which area of the Triangle of Sustainability is the most at risk?
- How can we strengthen it?
- If we were to start all over again today, given the resources that we now have in terms of people, fixed assets and funding, would we do it the same way?
- What is the biggest challenge we are likely to face in the next 3 years?
- What changes ought we to be making in our rolling Strategic Plan?

You have probably heard of the terms SWOT and PEST – no, I am not talking about flies and mosquitoes! They are both extremely useful tools in group exercises during these reviews. SWOT is an acronym for *Strengths, Weaknesses, Opportunities* and *Threats*. It is helpful to allow your team to brainstorm where they think your organisation is positioned according to these headings. What are you good at? What are you not so good at? Your strengths can also be weaknesses if considered from a different perspective. You will want to develop your strategic plan to play to your strengths, be aware of your weaknesses, grab new opportunities and watch out for threats. PEST stands for *Political, Economic, Sociological* and *Technological*. What might be happening in the political or economic worlds that you need to be preparing for? Do you need to be adapting to any social and technical changes? For instance, the rise in the use of social networking and 'smart phones' – how does this affect the way you should be interacting with your supporters? Remember that SWOT analysis will give you a snap shot of the current situation, whereas PEST is looking at future developments. You may want to bring in an outside facilitator to steer you though one of these sessions. Often, someone from outside the organisation will help you distinguish the wood from the trees.

It's all worthwhile

There will no doubt be times when you wondered why on earth you got into all this! Such is the calling of those of us dedicated to voluntary sector work. Very few of us chose this as a career. None of us expected to become wealthy as a result. But the rewards of seeing lives changed, of meeting human need, of seeing the world made into a better place for us all to live in, far surpass the temporary indulgences of salary and bonuses. Stay with it!

When I walk through park lands or some of the great estates, I wonder at the vision of those landscapers who laid out the design of magnificent trees, many of which would never achieve their full glory until generations after the designer had passed on. I am so thankful for men and women of vision who were prepared to invest their all for the sake of generations not yet imagined. *You are in that category.* You will probably never see the full results of the work you are now investing in. It will be there for others who come after you. So do it well, plant for future growth and success.

As the Roman general, Maximus, in Russell Crowe's epic movie *Gladiator* says:

'What we do in life echoes in eternity.' [4]

---

1 The RNIB has a web access centre on its website that gives advice on how to make your website accessible for partially sighted or blind people, with a simple procedure for testing your web pages. See www.rnib.org.uk

2 2010 prices.

3 www.cap.org.uk

4 Universal Pictures (2000).

Appendix: Registering a new charity

I never did answer Lisa's original question, *I'd like to register a charity. Where do I begin?* It may even be that in your case you are still at an earlier stage of contemplation; to take the plunge or not? Do you really want to take on all the legal and financial obligations of running a Registered Charity?

First of all, there is no such thing as a 'UK Registered Charity'. Charity law differs slightly between Scotland, Northern Ireland and that which applies in England and Wales. However, the Charity Commission for England and Wales website, www.charity-commission.gov.uk, is the place to start – it will also give details of the relevant offices for Scotland and Northern Ireland. The Charity Commission site is full of really useful information, even if you are not going to be based in England and Wales. It is written in no-nonsense language, and I have not attempted to repeat here what they have already so aptly provided. I simply want to highlight the process involved and some of the considerations you might want to bear in mind before you get started on the procedure.

Secondly, you cannot register your charity unless your turnover exceeds £5,000 per year. If your annual income is less than that, you can still call yourself a charity (albeit not a registered one) and, in theory at least, you are protected by charity law.

Advantages of registration
However, there are very clear advantages of registering:

- Having a registered charity number immediately gives credibility to your cause. Donors will know that you are regulated and that their donations must be used for the purposes you have described in your appeal literature or on your website. This is particularly important if your service delivery is expected to take place outside the UK. So if you are thinking of helping provide wells for a group of villages in West Africa, for instance, you would be best advised to register as a charity in the UK in order to increase donor confidence.

- Very few trusts or government bodies will consider making a grant to you unless you are registered.
- You can take advantage of tax-efficient donations. You cannot reclaim *Gift Aid* unless you are a registered charity, neither can you benefit from the *Give As You Earn* scheme.
- You can receive up to 80% relief on normal business rates on any buildings that you use for your charitable purposes.
- Charities do not have to pay Corporation Tax or any Stamp Duty Tax.
- If you are a registered charity, any gifts you receive are free from Inheritance Tax.
- Under certain circumstances, there are reductions on VAT for charities.

Types of charities

You will next need to decide what kind of charity you want to be. There are basically three main choices:

- Most small charities will want to be a *Charitable Trust*, unless they intend to engage in any significant trading activity and are not a membership-type of organisation. Setting up a Trust is the most straightforward option.
- A *Charitable Company* might be a better option for you if you want to generate income from trading. So if you are planning to offer services to the public for which a fee will be charged, or you are considering opening a number of charity shops, then this might be the right model for you. A charitable company is a private company limited by guarantee with objects that are charitable by law, as determined by the Charity Commission. Until the legal process for establishing a Charitable Incorporated Organisation (CIO) is resolved (see Chapter 6) you will first need to register your company with Companies House. This is quite straightforward and the forms can be downloaded from its website. There is a small fee for registering as a company. The second step is to register your company with the Charity Commission and obtain your charity number. There is no charge for this part.

- The third option is to form a Charitable Association. This is suitable if your organisation is going to be run for the benefit of and by the membership, and you do not intend to trade. The sorts of organisations that will opt for this route might be a local community group, or a former students' network of a college or school.

Deciding on which type of charity you want your organisation to be will determine the nature of your Governing Document. This is the formal document that lays down the purpose of the charity, how it is supposed to be run, and sets out who will be the trustees and what powers the charity has. The Charity Commission gives some sample Governing Documents which you can download and adapt to your own individual needs. If you choose to use one of their already-approved models, it speeds up the process of the application.

Bank account

Another prerequisite of the registration process is to open a bank account in the name of the charity. It must not be in your own name. You will need to show that you have had at least £5,000 turnover during the preceding 12 months. You can do this by submitting copies of bank statements. If you have not had the minimum £5,000 through your account, you will need to start on your initial fundraising straight away. Remember, if you are asking people to donate to your cause in order that you can register, you must explain that this is not a registration fee; the money belongs to your charity and will be used by you to achieve your charitable objects, so you can make it an attractive appeal. It cannot be a loan though – it must be made up of genuine donations.

Public benefit

The process of registering your charity is quite straightforward. The most difficult part for those who have never done it before is deciding how to express the *public benefits* that the charity will provide. The Charities Act 2006 requires all charities to have aims which are 'demonstrably' for the public benefit. I have had more than one client's registration held up because the trustees had not clearly 'demonstrated' how the public benefit was to be achieved. Again, there are very clear guidelines on this on the Charity Commission website.

Getting help with your registration

You may decide that this is all too complicated for you – it isn't that difficult really, but it can look daunting to the newcomer. If this is the case, you can find several organisations that will help you through the registration process. I have a flat rate fee which I charge for registration, which works out at less than the equivalent of two days' work. Sometimes it will take me longer than two days and, of course, the work is spread out over several weeks. The advantage of using someone like me to draft an application for you is that I know the wording that the Charity Commission has approved in the past, and I am familiar with the process they use. Do get in contact with me if you would like to discuss this further (www.givingthebest.co.uk).

Bibliography

Bruce, Ian, (1994) *Meeting Need: Successful Charity Marketing*, ICSA.

Belbin, R. Meredith, (1993) *Team Roles at Work*, Betterworth-Heinemann.

Burnett, Ken, (1992) *Relationship Fundraising*, White Lion Press.

Burnett, Ken, (1996) *Friends for Life*, White Lion Press.

Carver, John, (1997) *Boards that Make a Difference: A New Design for Leadership in Nonprofit and Public Organisations*, Josey-Bass.

Clarke, Sam and Norton, Michael, (1997) *The Complete Fundraising Handbook 3rd edition*, Directory of Social Change.

Courtney, Roger, (2002) *Strategic Management for Voluntary Non-profit Organisations*, Routledge.

Drucker, Peter F., (1995) *Managing the Non-Profit Organization*, Harper Collins.

Flory, Peter, (2004) *Fundraising Databases: An Introduction to the Setup and Use*, Wiremill Publishing.

Hofstede, Geert, (1991) *Cultures and Organisations: Software of the Mind*, McGraw-Hill.

Hughes, Bryn, (1998) *Leadership Tool Kit*, Monarch Books.

Johnson and Scholes, (1993) *Exploring Corporate Strategy: Text and Cases*, Prentice Hall International (UK).

Martin, Paul, (2008) *The Christian Charities Handbook: The Essential Guide for Trustees and Managers*, IVP.

McClelland, David, (1987) *Human Motivation*, Cambridge University Press.

Naisbitt, John, (1982) *Megatrends: 10 New Directions Transforming our Lives*, Warner Books.

Porter, M. E., (1997) *What is Strategy?* in S. Segal-Horn (ed) *The Strategic Reader*, Blackwell.

Index

Kenneth MacKenzie — expert on organisational structures.

pg 67 — words which sum up your charity

re trustees contact Aajiya Trust
The voice
How do we include S.U. I? Consult — or not ?!

Create "Purpose" + "Vision" statements
pg 61

AIM: to reach out to ethnic minority
grps more (AJ — useless!)
target groups — mailshot

Think who you can work with — isolated

groups
vision — visit so many businesses with seminars
receive so many enquiries
deliver so many talks / training
connected with so many people   pg 61